DAY-BY-DAY

WITH ANDREW MURRAY

Formerly published as
The Andrew Murray Yearbook

Compiled by
M. J. SHEPPERSON

Foreword by Armin R. Gesswein

Bethany Fellowship, Inc.
Minneapolis, Minnesota

Day-by-Day with Andrew Murray
Copyright 1961 by
Zondervan Publishing House

Printed in the United States of America
by the Printing Division of
Bethany Fellowship, Inc.
Minneapolis, Minnesota

FOREWORD

Andrew Murray still lives on! There is something very remarkable about his writings, for he has no great style, and hardly uses an illustration or story. Yet people of all kinds, no less than ministers, long for his words. I knew a very prominent businessman who, after a long and weary search in many cults, finally found Christ through the writings of Andrew Murray.

Andrew Murray was so close to Christ that, no matter what subject he presents, he seems to indwell it with Christ. In every line one feels his heart of love and his clear call of God to share his secrets of Christ as if they were hidden treasures. Whether he is writing on prayer, or obedience, or purity, or even perfection, his delight is not so much that of presenting a new subject. Rather, every subject is but a new way of presenting Christ.

I can't recall how this rare little volume came into my hands. It has long since been out of print. But here is a rare volume — full of golden nuggets. Here is a tremendous array of the best of Murray's many gems. Watch how each gem reflects some new facet of Christ!

I shared some of the secrets of this old volume at ministers' prayer conferences. At once men began to inquire, "Where can we get that book?" I said it is old and out of print. They said, "Can't you get it printed again? . . . I want to get it." This was something they had not said of other writings I shared with them.

May this new reprint bring to many thousands some of the great hidden riches of Christ discovered by this great saint of Christ!

ARMIN R. GESSWEIN, Director
Revival Prayer Fellowship, Inc.

Pasadena, Calif.

IN TIME OF TROUBLE SAY:

First —

He brought me here — it is by His will I am in this strait place; in that will I rest.

Next —

He will keep me in His love, and give me grace in this trial to behave as His child.

Then —

He will make the trial a blessing, teaching me the lessons He means me to learn, and working in me the grace He intends for me.

Last —

In His good time He can bring me out again, how and when He knows.

Say — I am here —

1. By God's appointment.
2. In God's keeping.
3. Under His training.
4. For His time.

ANDREW MURRAY

INTRODUCTION

I have been asked to write an introduction to a collection of extracts from my books. I gladly do so, as an acknowledgment of the love that has actuated the labour, and to bid the little book Godspeed on its way. When a servant of God knows that he has a message, however defective its delivery be, it is a joy to know that it has reached other hearts, and that it is by them being passed on farther.

If anyone asks me what that message has been, I think I may say honestly that it was nothing but this — that our Lord Jesus is willing to be far more to us than we know. All that we have enjoyed of Him is only a beginning. He is waiting to dispossess and deliver from the life of Self and self effort, and to let the life, and the light, and the love of God fill us, and be our life in a degree and a power we have very little idea of. For all that the Lord has allowed me to say of the possibility of Abiding in Him, of being Like Him, of entering with Him into the Secret of prayer and intercession, into the Holiest of All, I humbly praise Him. That in all things He may have the pre-eminence! — Let this be our watchword. Let an enthusiastic devotion to His service, let an absolute and unceasing dependence upon His presence and working prove that He is All in all to us. As the soul turns from itself and the creature to allow Him to become its life, it will begin to know what it was God created us for, and to be fitted for more effectually passing on to others that life which it has in Him.

With my loving greetings to the compiler and all her readers,

Ever yours in Christ Jesus,
ANDREW MURRAY

November 2, 1898

CONTENTS

DAY-BY-DAY with
ANDREW MURRAY

1 When you get a promise from God, it is worth just as
   much as a fulfilment. Only honour Him by trusting the
promise and obeying Him, and any preparation that you still
need, God knows about; if there is anything that is to be
opened up to you, He will do it, if you count upon Him to
do it. Do not look to what we say or to what you think and
understand. Look to God, and expect God to do something.

The true taking away of sin is this: If the light comes in,
the darkness is expelled. It is the presence of Jesus indwelling by the Holy Spirit that can make us holy.

The Spirit did all on the day of Pentecost and afterwards.
It was the Spirit who gave the boldness, the wisdom, the
message, the converting power.

*   *   *

2 Let everyone who longs for the blessing of the Spirit
   take these four little words as steps: — I must be filled;
I may be filled; I would be filled; I shall be filled.

What is obedience? Giving up my will to the will of another. Christ said, "Not my will, but Thine be done." Jesus
gave up His life to God, and thereby taught us that the only
thing that life is worth living for is to give it back to God,
even unto death.

Christ could never have ascended to sit upon the throne,
never could have accomplished His work of preparing the
Kingdom that He could give to the Father, if He had not
begun by giving up *Himself,* and let God do all.

*   *   *

3 The throne in heaven is not the throne of the Lamb of
   God alone; it is the throne of God and the Lamb. Jesus
went to share the throne with the Father. The Father was
always the first and Jesus the second.

There are two spirits on earth. Paul said, "We have received not the spirit of the world, but the Spirit that is of
God." That is the great want in every worker — the spirit of

11

the world going out, and the Spirit of God coming in to take possession of the inner life and of the whole being.

Oh, what fellowship! The Holy Spirit in heaven doing part of the work, man on earth doing the other part. After the ordination of the men upon earth, it is written in God's inspired Word that they were sent forth by the Holy Ghost.

* * *

4 Jesus said to Peter, "Deny thyself," and again, "Thou wilt deny me." There is no choice for us; we must either deny self or deny Christ.

It is when the individual workers are blessed that the work will prosper, and the body be in health and strength.

Before God took His Son up to heaven, He let Him live here upon earth, that in His life I might have a complete representation of what my God wanted me to be and was willing to make me.

Absolute surrender! How am I to live that life? The Father points to the beloved Son, and says, "This is My beloved Son, in whom I am well pleased." Hear Him, follow Him, live like Him, let Christ be the rule of your life.

Deliverance from the self-life means to be a vessel overflowing with love to everybody all the day.

* * *

5 If a vessel that ought to be one whole is cracked into many pieces, it cannot be filled. You can take out one part and dip out a little water, but if you want the vessel full, the vessel must be whole. This is true of Christ's church. If there is one thing we have to pray for, it is this: Lord, melt us together into One by the power of the Holy Spirit.

The will of the creature is nothing but an empty vessel in which the power of God is to be made manifest.

God does not work by His Spirit as He works by a blind force in nature. He leads His people on as reasonable, intelligent beings; and, therefore, when we have come to the end of self, to the conviction that though we have been striv-

12

ing to obey the law, we have failed, then He shows us that in the Holy Spirit we have the power of obedience, victory, real holiness.

* * *

6 When a question is asked, an answer is expected. Alas, how many Christians are content with the question, "O wretched man that I am! Who shall deliver me from the body of this death?" Instead of saying, "I thank God through Jesus Christ our Lord," they are forever repeating the question without the answer.

God has called the Church of Christ to live in the power of the Holy Spirit, and the Church is living for the most part in the power of human flesh, and of will and energy and effort apart from the Spirit of God. If the Church will return to acknowledge that the Holy Spirit is her strength and her help, to give up everything and wait upon God to be filled with the Spirit, her days of beauty and gladness will return, and we shall see the glory of God revealed amongst us.

* * *

7 I have often been asked by young Christians, "Why is it that I fail so? I did so solemnly vow with my whole heart and did desire to serve God. Why have I failed?" You are trying to do in your own strength what Christ alone can do in you. You were trusting in yourself, or you could not have failed. If you had trusted Christ, He could not fail.

You cannot work out God's will, but His Holy Spirit can; and until the Church, until believers grasp this, and cease trying by human effort to do God's will, and wait upon the Holy Spirit to come with all His omnipotent and enabling power, the Church will never be what God wants her to be, and what God is willing to make of her.

We find the Christian life so difficult because we seek for God's blessing, while we live in our own will. We make our

own plans and choose our own work, and then we ask Him
to give us His blessing.

*   *   *

8 You may have ten hours' hard work daily, during which
your brain has to be occupied with temporal things; God
orders it so. But abiding in Jesus is the work of the heart,
not of the brain, the heart clinging to and resting in Jesus;
a work in which the Holy Spirit links us to Jesus. Deeper
down than the brain, deep down in the inner life, you can
abide in Christ, so that every moment you are free the consciousness will come: Blessed Jesus, I am still in Thee.

Do not confound work and fruit. There may be a good
deal of work for Christians that is not the fruit of the Heavenly Vine. Do not seek for work only. Fruit-bearing means
the very life and power and spirit and love within the heart
of the Son of God — the Heavenly Vine Himself coming into
your heart and mine.

*   *   *

9 God hath begotten us to an inheritance incorruptible,
reserved in heaven for you, who are kept by the power
of God. My God is keeping the inheritance for me, and
keeping me for the inheritance. The same power, the same
love, the same God doing the double work.

I have a watch borrowed from a friend. I injure the watch;
the hands are broken, face defaced, some of the wheels and
springs spoiled, and I take it back in that condition. My
friend would say, "I did not want you to keep my watch so
that you should bring me back only the shell of the watch.
I expected you to keep every part of it." So God does not
want to keep us in this general way, so that we shall just get
into heaven; but the keeping power and love of God applies
to every particular of our being.

*   *   *

14

10 The altar sanctifies the gift. Christ is not only the Priest and the Victim, but the Living Christ is Himself the Altar. All unworthy and all feeble though I be, the altar sanctifies the gift, and in Jesus and resting on Him, my God accepts my feebleness, and I am well pleasing in His sight.

Do you see yonder clock? If I see that the hands stand still, and point wrong, and that the clock is slow or fast, I say that there is something inside the clock that is wrong. Temper is like the revelation that the clock gives of what is within — is a proof of whether the love of Christ is filling the heart.

* * *

11 Does it cost the lamb any trouble to be gentle? No, it is its nature. Why does it cost a wolf no trouble to be cruel, and to put its fangs into the poor lamb? Because that is its nature. How can I learn to love? Never, until the Spirit of God fills my heart with God's love.

There is a difference between the power of the Spirit as a gift and the power of the Spirit for the grace of a holy life. A man may often have a measure of the power of the Spirit, but if there be not a large measure of the Spirit as the Spirit of grace and of holiness, the defect will be manifest in his work.

* * *

12 On the day of Pentecost the Holy Spirit came, and Peter was a changed man. When he said to Christ, "Thou never canst suffer," he had not a conception of what it was to pass through death into life. When I hear him say, "If ye be reproached for the name of Christ, happy are ye, for the Spirit of God and of glory resteth upon you," that is not the old Peter, but the very Spirit of Christ breathing and speaking within him.

Suppose that when a painter came into his studio to paint an unfinished picture, the canvas always removed to some other part of the room. Of course the painter could not paint.

Suppose the canvas to say, "O painter, I will be still; come and paint thy beautiful picture." Then the painter would come and do it. Say to God, "Thou art the wondrous artist. I am still. I trust Thy power." God will then work wonders with you. God never works anything but wonders.

*   *   *

13 Your religious life is every day to be a proof that God works impossibilities; your religious life is to be a series of impossibilities made possible and actual by God's Almighty power. I do not want a little of God's power, but I want — with reverence be it said — the whole of God's omnipotence to keep me right and make me live like a Christian.

Is it not often true that our work comes between us and Jesus? Sad thought that the bearing of fruit should separate the branch from the vine. That must be because we have looked upon our work as something else than the branch bearing fruit.

I thank God for the interest that He is awakening in foreign missions, in drunkards, in the poor outcast; but your middle classes, your richer and higher classes, — is there no power in your duty to take the gospel to them boldly?

*   *   *

THE TRUE VINE

14 All that Christ is and has, He has, not in Himself, but from the Father. Before He ever uses the word, or speaks at all of abiding in Him, or bearing fruit, Christ turns their eyes heavenward to the Father watching over them, and working all in them. The great lack of the Christian life is that, even where we trust Christ, we leave God out of the count. Christ came to bring us to God. Christ lived the life of a man exactly as we have to live it. Christ, the Vine, points to God, the Husbandman.

*   *   *

15   Think of the vine first:—The branch has but one object
         for which it exists, one purpose to which it is entirely
given up, — to bear the fruit the vine wishes to bring forth.
And so the believer has but one reason for his being a branch
— but one reason for his existence on earth — that the Heavenly Vine may through Him bring forth His fruit. Second:—
The branch is exactly like the vine in every aspect — the same
nature, the same life, the same place, the same work. In all
this they are inseparably one. And so the believer needs to
know that he is partaker of the Divine nature, and has the
very nature and Spirit of Christ in him, and that his one
calling is to yield himself to a perfect conformity to Christ.
Third:—The vine has its stores of life and sap and strength,
not for itself, but for the branches. The branches are and
have nothing but what the vine provides and imparts. The
branch has but to yield itself and receive. This truth leads
to the blessed rest of faith, the true secret of growth and
strength: "I can do all things through Christ which strengtheneth me."

                         *   *   *

16   Ere we begin to think of fruit or branches, let us have
         our heart filled with the faith: as glorious as the Vine
is the Husbandman. As high and holy is our calling, so mighty
and loving is the God who will work it all. As surely as the
Husbandman made the Vine what it was to be, will He make
each Branch what it is to be. Many Christians think their
own salvation is the first thing; their temporal life the second;
and what is left of time and interest may be devoted to fruit-
bearing to the saving of men; in most cases, very little time
or interest can be found. The one condition of my abiding
and growing strong is that I bear the fruit of the Heavenly
Vine for dying men to eat and live.

                         *   *   *

17   As churches and individuals, we are in danger of noth-
         ing so much as self-contentment. The secret spirit of

Laodicea—we are rich and increased in goods, and have need of nothing — may prevail where not suspected. The Divine warning — poor and wretched and miserable — finds little response just where most needed. Let us not rest content with the thought that we are taking an equal share with others in the work, or that men are satisfied with our efforts. Let our only desire be to know whether we are bearing all the fruit Christ is willing to give through us as living Branches, in close and living union with Himself.

*   *   *

18 What a solemn, precious lesson! It is not to sin only that the cleansing of the Husbandman refers. It is to our own religious activity, as it is developed in the very act of bearing fruit. In working for God our natural gifts of wisdom, or eloquence, or influence, or zeal are ever in danger of being unduly developed, and then trusted in. So, after each season of work, God has to bring us to the end of ourselves, to the consciousness of the helplessness and the danger of all that is of man, to feel that we are nothing. All that is to be left of us is just enough to receive the power of the life-giving sap of the Holy Spirit. What is of man must be reduced to its very lowest measure. All that is inconsistent with the most entire devotion to Christ's service must be removed. The more perfect the cleansing and cutting away of all that is of self, the less of surface over which the Holy Spirit is to be spread, so much the more intense can be the concentration of our whole being, to be entirely at the disposal of the Spirit.

*   *   *

19 Many believers pray and long very earnestly for the filling of the Spirit and the indwelling of Christ, and wonder that they do not make more progress. The reason is often this: the "I in you" cannot come because the "Abide in Me" is not maintained. "There is one body and one spirit"; before the Spirit can fill, there must be a body prepared. The graft must have grown into the stem and be abiding in it before the sap can flow through to bring forth fruit. It is as in lowly obedience we follow Christ, even in external things, denying ourselves, forsaking the world, and even in the body seeking to be conformable to Him, as we thus seek to abide in Him, that we shall be able to receive and enjoy the "I in you." The work enjoined on us, "Abide in Me," will prepare us for the work undertaken by Him, "I in you."

The vision of Christ is an irresistible attraction; it draws and holds us like a magnet. Listen ever to the living Christ still speaking to you, and waiting to show you the meaning and power of His word, *"I am the Vine."* So it sometimes comes, that souls who have never been specially occupied with the thought of abiding, are abiding all the time, because they are occupied with Christ.

*   *   *

20 Have you ever noticed the difference in the Christian life between work and fruit? A machine can do work; only life can bear fruit. A law can compel work; only life can spontaneously bring forth fruit. Work implies effort and labour; the essential idea of fruit is, that it is the silent, natural, restful produce of our inner life. The connection between work and fruit is, perhaps, best seen in the expression, "fruitful in every good work" (Col. 1:10). It is only when good works come as the fruit of the indwelling Spirit that they are acceptable to God. Under the compulsion of law and conscience, or the influence of inclination and zeal, men may be most diligent in good works, and yet find that they have but little spiritual result. Their works are man's effort, instead of being the fruit of the Spirit, the restful, natural outcome of the Spirit's operation within us.

*   *   *

21 A deep conviction of the truth of this word, "Except ye abide in Me, ye can do nothing," lies at the very root of a strong spiritual life. As little as I created myself, as little as I could raise a man from the dead, can I give myself the Divine life, maintain or increase it: every motion is the work of God through Christ and His Spirit. As a man believes this, he will take up that position of entire and continual dependence which is the very essence of the life of faith. His whole heart says Amen to the word, "You can do nothing." And just because he does so, he can also say, "I can do all things in Christ who strengtheneth me."

* * *

22 We can only fulfil our calling to bear much fruit by praying much. In Christ are hid all the treasures men around us need; in Him all God's children are blessed with all spiritual blessings; He is full of grace and truth. But it needs prayer, much prayer, strong believing prayer, to bring these blessings down. We cannot appropriate the promise in John 15:7, without a life given up for men.

* * *

23 There have always been a smaller number of God's people who have sought to serve Him with their whole heart, while the majority have been content with a very small measure of the knowledge of His grace and will.

And what is the difference between this smaller inner circle and the many who do not seek admission to it? We find it in the words, "much fruit." With many Christians the thought of personal safety, which, at their first awakening was a legitimate one, remains to the end the one aim of their religion. The idea of service and fruit is always a secondary and very subordinate one. We see in God's Word everywhere these two classes of disciples. Let our desire be nothing less than perfect cleansing, unbroken abiding, closest communion, abundant fruitfulness, — true Branches of the True Vine.

* * *

24 Some have told of a wonderful change, by which their life of continual failure and stumbling had been changed into a very blessed experience of being kept and strengthened and made exceeding glad. If you asked them how this great blessing came to them, many would tell you it was simply this: that they were led to believe that this abiding in Christ's love was meant to be a reality, and that they were made willing to give up everything for it, and then enabled to trust Christ to make it true to them. The feebleness of our Christian life is that we do not take time to believe that this Divine love does really delight in us, and will possess and work all in us. We do not take time to look at the Vine bearing the Branch so entirely, working all in it so completely. We strive to do for ourselves what Christ alone can, what Christ, oh! so lovingly, longs to do for us.

*   *   *

25 Through His will, loved and done, lies the path to His love. A sin of ignorance has still the nature of sin. God will deal with this in due time in the way of searching and humbling, and, if we be simple and faithful, give us larger deliverance than we dare expect. Obedience has reference to the positive keeping of the commandments of our Lord, and the performance of His will in everything in which we know it. It is the whole-hearted surrender in everything to do His will that gives access to a life in the abiding enjoyment of His love. It is only through knowing God's will one can know His heart, and only through doing that will one can abide in His love.

*   *   *

26 God's will is the very centre of His Divine perfection. As revealed in His commandments, it opens up the way for the creature to grow into the likeness of the Creator. In accepting and doing His will, I rise into fellowship with Himself. Therefore it was that the Son, when coming into the world spoke: "I come to do Thy will, O God!" This was the place, and this would be the blessedness of the creature. This was what he had lost in the Fall. This was what Christ came to restore. This is what, as the Heavenly Vine, He asks of us and imparts to us, that even as He, by keeping His Father's commandments, abode in His love, we should keep His commandments and abide in His love.

* * *

27 The Word is God's pruning knife, sharper than any two-edged sword that pierces even to the dividing asunder of the soul and spirit, and is quick to discern the thoughts and intents of the heart. Only when affliction leads to the Word does it become a blessing; the lack of this heart-cleansing through the Word is the reason why affliction is so often unsanctified. Jesus says, "Ye are already clean, because of the Word I have spoken unto you." It is as the soul gives up its own thoughts and men's thoughts of what is religion, and yields itself heartily, humbly, patiently, to the teaching of the Word by the Spirit, that the Father will do His blessed work of pruning and cleansing away all of nature and self that mixes with our work and hinders His Spirit. If anyone asks, "How can I be a happy Christian?" our Lord's answer is very simple: "These things," about the Vine and the Branches, "I have spoken to you that My joy may be in you, and that your joy may be fulfilled." You cannot have My joy without My life. Abide in Me, and let Me abide in you, and My joy will be in you. All healthy life is a thing of joy and beauty; live undividedly the Branch life; you will have His joy in full measure.

* * *

28 To many Christians the thought of a life wholly abiding in Christ is one of strain and painful effort. The strain and effort only come as long as we do not yield ourselves unreservedly to the life of Christ in us. The very first words of the parable are not yet opened up to them: "I am the True Vine; I undertake all and provide for all; I ask nothing of the Branch but that it yields wholly to Me, and allows Me to do all. I engage to make and keep the Branch all that it ought to be."

22

Salvation is nothing but love conquering and entering into us; we have just as much of salvation as we have of love. Full salvation is perfect love. There is no knowing God but by having the life; the life working in us alone gives the knowledge. And even so, the love; if we would know it, we must drink of its living stream, we must have it shed forth by the Holy Spirit in us.

*   *   *

29 As we know His dying love, we shall joyfully obey its commands; as we obey the commands, we shall know the love more fully. The imperative necessity of obedience, doing all that Christ commands us, has not the place in our Christian teaching and living that Christ meant it to have. We have given a far higher place to privilege than to duty. We have not considered implicit obedience as a condition of true discipleship. The secret thought that it is impossible to do the things He commands us, and that therefore it cannot be expected of us, a subtle and unconscious feeling that sinning is a necessity, has frequently robbed both precepts and promises of their power. Let us take Christ's words as most literally true, and make nothing less the law of our life. "Ye are My friends if ye do the things that I command you."

*   *   *

30 Throughout Scripture this is the great object of the teaching of election. — "Predestinated to be conformed to the image of His Son" (to be Branches in the image and likeness of the Vine). "Chosen that we should be holy." "Chosen to salvation through sanctification of the Spirit." "Elect in sanctification of the Spirit unto obedience." In John 15:16, Christ reveals His two-fold purpose in choosing us to be His Branches: that we may bear fruit on earth, and have power in prayer in heaven.

*   *   *

31 Are you leaving your mark for eternity on those around
you? It is not your preaching or teaching, your strength
of will or power to influence, that will secure this. All depends
on having your life full of God and His power. And that
again depends upon your living the truly Branch-like life of
abiding — very close and unbroken fellowship with Christ.
It is the Branch that abides in Him that brings forth much
fruit — fruit that will abide. It is because we so little live
the true Branch life, because we so little lose ourselves in the
Vine, abiding in Him entirely, that we feel so little constrained
to much prayer, so little confident that we shall be heard, and
so do not know how to use His name as the key of God's
storehouse. The power of direct access to the Father for
men, the liberty of intercession, claiming and receiving blessing for them in faith, is the highest exercise of our union with
Christ. Let all who would truly and fully be Branches give
themselves to the work of intercession. It is the one great
work of Christ, the Vine in heaven, the source of power for
all His work. Make it your one great work as Branch: it
will be the power of all your work.

1 If in our orthodox Churches the living union with Christ, the experience of His daily and hourly presence and keeping, were preached with the same distinction and urgency as His atonement, many would be found to accept with gladness the invitation to such a life, and its influence would be manifest in their experience of the purity and the power, the love and the joy, the fruit-bearing, and all the blessedness which the Saviour connected with the abiding in Him.

* * *

2 We all know the need of time for our meals each day. If we are to live through Jesus, we must thoroughly take in and assimilate that heavenly food the Father has given us in His life. My brother who would learn to abide in Jesus, take time each day to put yourself into living contact with the living Jesus, to yield yourself distinctly and consciously to His blessed influence; so will you give him the opportunity of taking hold of you, of drawing you up and keeping you safe in His almighty life.

* * *

3 Jesus gives rest in Him — the rest of pardon and acceptance, the rest in His love. But we know that all that God bestows needs time to become fully our own; it must be held fast, and appropriated and assimilated into our inmost being; without this not even Christ's giving can make it our very own, in full experience and enjoyment.

* * *

4 Giving up one's whole life to Him, for Him alone to rule and order it; taking up His yoke and submitting to be led and taught; to learn of Him; abiding in Him, to be and do only what He wills, — these are the conditions of discipleship, without which there can be no thought of maintaining the rest that was bestowed on first coming to Christ. The Christian's rest is in Christ, and not of the Christian. He gives it not apart from Himself, and so it is only in having Him that the rest can really be kept and enjoyed.

5 Consecration and faith are the essential elements of the
Christian life, the giving up all to Jesus, the receiving all
from Jesus. They are implied in each other; they are united
in the one word — surrender.

* * *

6 Abiding in Him is not a work that we have to do as the
condition for enjoying His salvation, but a consenting to
let Him do all for us.

* * *

7 It was because Paul knew that the Mighty and the Faithful One had grasped him with the glorious purpose of
making him one with Himself, that he did his utmost to grasp
the glorious prize.

* * *

8 As a prophet, Christ is our wisdom, revealing to us God
and His love, with the nature and conditions of the salvation that love has prepared. As a priest, He is our righteousness, restoring us to right relations to God, and securing
us His favour and friendship. As a king, He is our sanctification, forming and guiding us into the obedience to the Father's
holy will. As these three offices work out God's purpose, the
grand consummation will be reached, the complete deliverance from sin and all its effects be accomplished, and ran-
somed humanity regain all that it had ever lost.

* * *

9 What we do is only the manifestation of what God is
doing in us; but the grace the promise offered is so large,
so God-like, so beyond all our thoughts, that we do not take
it really to mean what it says.

* * *

10 The believer knows himself to be in the school of God,
a Teacher who plans the whole course of study for each
of His pupils with infinite wisdom, and delights to have them

come daily for the lessons He has to give. All the believer asks is to feel himself constantly in God's hands, and to follow His guidance, neither lagging behind nor going before.

* * *

11 For the sanctifying of our memory in the service of our spiritual life, God has provided most bountifully; the Holy Spirit is—blessed be God—the memory of the new man. It is as we see what Jesus is, and is to us, that the abiding in Him will become the natural and spontaneous result of our knowledge of Him.

* * *

12 Each blessed experience we receive as a gift of God must at once be returned back to Him from whom it came in praise and love, in self-sacrifice and service; so only can it be restored to us again, fresh and beautiful with the bloom of heaven.

* * *

13 Whether we look backward and see the work He has done, or upward and see the reward He has in the Father's love that passeth knowledge, or forward in the continual accessions of joy as sinners are brought home, His joy is ours.

* * *

14 Our difficulties all arise from the want of the full surrender to a full abiding. Do thou but yield up thyself to Christ thy Lord, the conquering power of His incoming presence will make it joy to cast out all that before was most precious. "A hundredfold in this life": this word of the Master comes true to all who with whole-hearted faithfulness accept His commands to forsake all.

* * *

15 The heart occupied with its own plans and efforts for doing God's will and securing the blessing of abiding in Jesus must fail continually. God can do His work perfectly

27

only when the soul ceases from its work. He will do His work mightily in the soul that honours Him by expecting Him to work both to will and to do.

* * *

16 Christ was the revelation of the Father on earth. Believers are the revelation of Christ on earth. They cannot be this unless there be perfect unity, so that the world can know that he loves them and has sent them. But they can be it if Christ loves them with infinite love that gives itself and all it has, and if they abide in that love.

* * *

17 The secret of a life of close abiding will be seen to be simply this: As I give myself wholly to Christ, I find the power to take Him wholly for myself; and as I lose myself and all I have for Him, He takes me wholly for Himself, and gives Himself wholly to me.

Let a living faith in Christ working in you be the secret spring of all your work.

* * *

18 The believer who studies this life of Christ as the pattern and the promise of what his may be, learns to understand how the "Without Me, ye can do nothing," is but the forerunner of "I can do all things through Christ who strengtheneth me." We learn to glory in infirmities, to take pleasure in necessities and distresses for Christ's sake; for "When I am weak, then am I strong."

* * *

19 In the life of Divine love, the emptying of self and the sacrifice of our will is the surest way to have all we can wish or will. Dependence, subjection, self-sacrifice are for the Christian, as for Christ, the blessed path of life. Like as Christ lived through and in the Father, even so the believer, in and through Christ.

28

20   To him who is really seeking to abide in Christ's love, the commands become no less precious than the promises. As much as the promises they are the revelation of the Divine love, blessed helpers in the path to a closer union with the Lord.

* * *

21   No sooner is the doing of God's will to the Christian what Scripture and the Holy Spirit reveal it to be — the restoration to communion with God and conformity to Him, — than he feels that there is no law more natural or more beautiful than this: Keeping Christ's commandments the way to abide in Christ's love.

* * *

22   The weakest believer may be confident that in asking to be kept from sin, to grow in holiness, to bring forth much fruit, he may count upon these his petitions being fulfilled with Divine power. The power is in Jesus; Jesus is ours, with all His fulness; it is in us, His members, that the power is to work and to be made manifest.

* * *

23   The promise, "Whatsoever ye ask in My name," may not be severed from the commandment, "Whatsoever ye do, do all in the name of the Lord Jesus." If the name of Christ is to be wholly at my disposal, I must first put myself wholly at His disposal, so that He has full and free command of me. It is the abiding in Christ that gives the right and power to use His name with confidence.

* * *

24   We have each day to be faithful for the one short day, and long years and a long life take care of themselves, without the sense of their length or their weight ever being a burden. The single days do indeed make up the whole life, and the value of each single day depends on its influence on the whole.

25 Abiding by faith in Christ our sanctification is the simple secret of a holy life. The measure of sanctification will depend on the measure of abiding in Him; as the soul learns wholly to abide in Christ, the promise is increasingly fulfilled: "The very God of peace sanctify you wholly."

* * *

26 As our communion with Him becomes more intimate and intense, and we let the Holy Spirit reveal Him to us in His heavenly glory, the more we realise how the life in us is the life of One who sits upon the throne of heaven. We feel the power of an endless life working in us. We taste the eternal life. We have the foretaste of the eternal glory.

* * *

27 Not only is what is given up to Christ received back again to become doubly our own, but the forsaking all is followed by the receiving all. We abide in Christ more fully as we forsake all and follow Him. As I count all things loss for His sake, I am found in HIM.

* * *

28 In Him thou seest a thousand times more given thee than thou hast lost; seest how God only took from thee that thou mightest have room to take from Him what is so much better.

When thou seest affliction coming, meet it in Christ; when it is come, feel that thou art more in Christ than in it, for He is nearer thee than affliction ever can be; when it is passing, still abide in Him.

* * *

29 Our daily life must have for its object the making of an impression favourable to Jesus. When you look at the branch, you see at once the likeness to the vine. We must live so that somewhat of the holiness and the gentleness of Jesus may shine out in us. We must live to represent Him.

Work for Christ has sometimes drawn away from Christ, and taken the place of fellowship with Him.

1 To study the image of God in the Man Christ Jesus, to yield and set open our inmost being for that image to take possession and live in us, and then to go forth and let the heavenly likeness reflect itself and shine out in our life among our fellow-men, — this is what we have been redeemed for; let this be what we live for.

* * *

2 The reason why we so often do not bless others is that we wish to address them as their superiors in grace or gifts, or, at least, their equals. The love of Christ flowing into you will flow again from you, and make it your greatest joy to follow His example in washing the feet of others.

* * *

3 The external and bodily is the gate to the inner and spiritual life. He makes the salvation of the soul the first object in His holy ministry of love; at the same time, however, seeking the way to the hearts by the ready service of love in the little and common things of daily life.

* * *

4 Because my Surety is not someone outside of me, but One in whom I am, and who is in me, therefore it is that I can become like Him. He lives Himself in me. To follow His footsteps is a duty, because it is a possibility, the natural result of the wonderful union between Head and Members. I have to gaze on His example so as to know and follow it; and to abide in Him and open my heart to the blessed workings of His life in me.

* * *

5 As surely as Jesus conquered sin and its curse for me, will He conquer it in its power in me. What He began by His death for me, He will perfect by His life in me.

* * *

6 Taking up the cross and following Jesus is nothing less than living every day with our own life and will given up to death. The crucified Christ and the crucified Christian

31

belong to each other. The Christian glories in the cross because it makes him a partner in a death and victory that has already been accomplished, and in which the deliverance from the powers of the flesh and of the world has been secured to him.

*   *   *

7 The Lord Jesus has shown us that the best place to practise self-denial is in our ordinary intercourse with men.

*   *   *

8 Who can say whether this is not one of the secrets which eternity will reveal, that sin was permitted because otherwise God's love could never so fully have been revealed? The highest glory of God's love was manifest in the self-sacrifice of Christ. Without entire self-sacrifice we cannot love as Jesus loved.

*   *   *

9 It is only when we sacrifice ourselves to God that there will be the power for an entire self-sacrifice. When faith has first appropriated the promise, "Inasmuch as ye have done it unto the least of these My brethren, ye have done it unto Me," I understand the glorious harmony between sacrifice to God and sacrifice for men.

*   *   *

10 The freer the Church is of the spirit and principles of the world, the more influence she will exert in it. The believer sees that the only way to answer to his calling is, as crucified to the world, to withdraw himself from its power, as living in Christ to go into it and bless it. He lives in heaven and walks on earth.

*   *   *

11 The Church of Christ in her mission, "Go ye and teach all nations," has the promise, "Lo, I am with you always." The Lord does not demand anything which He does not give the power to perform. The Lord Jesus will give His people all the preparation they need.

12 Christ's mission is the only reason for our being on earth. Just as with Jesus, our heavenly mission demands nothing less than entire consecration.

* * *

13 The stronger the Christian's faith is in God's everlasting purpose, the more his courage for work will be strengthened; the more he works and is blessed, the clearer it will become that all is of God.

* * *

14 The great object of redemption was to make us and our will free from the power of sin, and to lead us again to live and do the will of God. In His life on earth He showed us what it is to live only for the will of God; in His death and resurrection He won for us the power to live and do the will of God as He had done.

* * *

15 Not herein is sin, that man has a creature will different from the Creator's, but in this, that he clings to his own will when it is seen to be contrary to the will of the Creator. Take God's will as one great whole, as the only thing for which you live on earth.

* * *

16 God's will only seems hard as we look at it from a distance, and are unwilling to submit to it. How beautiful the will of God makes everything in Nature! The will of God is the will of His love. How can you fear to surrender yourself to it?

* * *

17 A hearty obedience to the commandments, and a ready obedience to the conscience, are the preparation for that Divine teaching of the Spirit which will lead thee deeper into the meaning and application of the Word, and into a more direct and spiritual insight into God's will with regard to thyself personally. It is to those *who obey* Him, God gives the Holy Spirit, through whom the blessed will of God becomes

33

the light that shines evermore brightly on our path! — "If any man will do His will, he shall know."

* * *

18 A Christlike sense of sonship will lead to a Christlike obedience.

* * *

19 It was the compassionate sympathy of Jesus that attracted so many to Him upon earth; that same compassionate tenderness will still, more than anything, draw souls to you and your Lord.

* * *

20 Just in proportion as we live in more or less entire dependence on the Father, will His life plan for us be more or less perfectly worked out in our lives. The nearer the believer comes to this entire dependence of the Son, doing nothing but what He sees the Father do, and then to His implicit obedience, whatsoever He doeth, doing these in like manner, so much more will the promise be fulfilled in us. The Father showeth him all things that He Himself doeth, and will show him greater works than these.

* * *

21 The desire for independence was the temptation in Paradise, is the temptation in each human heart. It seems hard to be nothing, to know nothing, to will nothing. And yet it is so blessed. This dependence brings us into most blessed communion with God; it takes from us all care and responsibility. It gives us real power and strength of will, because we know that He works in us to will and to do. It gives us the blessed assurance that our work will succeed, because we have allowed God alone to take charge of it.

* * *

22 Just because Jesus' life was strong and true, it could not bear the loss of direct and constant intercourse with the Father, with whom and in whom it had its being, and its blessedness. Even work in the service of God and

of love is exhausting; we cannot bless others without power
going out from us; this must be renewed from above. It is
from Heaven alone that the power to lead a heavenly life
on earth can come.

* * *

23   The entire sacrifice of ourselves to God in every prayer
of daily life is the only preparation for those single
hours of soul-struggle in which we may be called to some
special act of the surrender of the will that costs us tears and
anguish. But he who has learnt the former, will surely receive strength for the latter.

* * *

24   When we behold the glory of God in Christ, in the
glass of the Holy Scriptures, His glory shines upon us,
and into us, and fills us, until it shines out from us again.
Beholding Jesus makes us like Him.

* * *

25   It is grace we need, and not sin, to make and keep us
humble. The heaviest laden branches always bow the
lowest. The nearer the soul comes to God, the more His
Majestic Presence makes it feel its littleness.

* * *

26   If the believer holds fast what his participation with
Christ's death signifies, he has the power to overcome
sin. It is not said sin is dead; but he himself is dead to sin and
alive to God, and so sin cannot for a single moment, without
his consent, have dominion over him. If he sin, it is because
he allows it to reign, and submits himself to it.

* * *

27   How many have been looking most earnestly for the
full insight into the blessedness of being "dead unto
sin and alive unto God," and yet have failed. They have been
more occupied with the blessings to be had in Jesus, or with

the effort to exercise a strong abiding faith in these blessings as theirs, than with Jesus Himself, in whom both the blessings and the faith that sees them are ours.

* * *

28 It is as you bear the image of God here, as you live in the likeness of Jesus, who is the brightness of His glory, and the express image of His person, that you will be fitted for the glory to come. If we are to bear the image of the heavenly, the Christ in glory, we must first bear the image of the earthly, the Christ in humiliation.

* * *

29 To be filled with the Holy Spirit we must wait on our Lord in faith. His love desires to give us more than we know. You are in the Spirit as your vital air; the Spirit is in you as your life-breath. It is impossible to say what the Lord Jesus would do for a soul who is truly willing to live as entirely through Him, as He is through the Father.

* * *

30 With what care the tenderly sensitive plate of the photographer is prepared to receive the impression; with what precaution its relative position to the object to be portrayed is adjusted; how still and undisturbed it is then held face to face with that object. Having done this, the photographer leaves the light to do its wonderful work; his work is a work of faith. Let us believe in the power of the light of God to transcribe Christ's image on our heart. Let us not seek to do the work the Spirit must do. Let us simply trust Him to do it. Our duty is to seek the prepared heart waiting, longing, praying for the likeness; to take our place face to face with Jesus, gazing, loving, believing that the wonderful vision of that Crucified One is the sure promise of what we can be; then putting aside all that can distract, in stillness of soul, silent unto God, just to allow the blessed Spirit as the light of God to do the work.

31   Himself for us; us for Himself; an entire exchange; a perfect union; a complete identity in interest and purpose. Himself for us, as Saviour; us for Himself, still as Saviour, like Him and for Him to continue on earth the work which He began.

1 Each of us must learn that there is a Holiest of All in
that temple which he himself is; the secret place of the
Most High within us must become the central truth in our
temple worship. This must be the meaning of our confession: "I believe in the Holy Ghost."

* * *

2 Love every believer, not for the sake of what in him is
in sympathy with thee or pleasing to thee, but for the
sake of the Spirit of the Father which is in him.

* * *

3 The fuller the Spirit's indwelling and the mightier His
working is, the more truly spiritual your being becomes,
the more will self sink away, and the Spirit of Christ use you
in building up and building together believers into a habitation of God.

* * *

4 The trust in gifts and knowledge, in soundness of creed
and earnestness of work, the satisfaction in forms and
services, leaves the flesh in full vigour, not crucified with
Christ, and so the Spirit is not free to work out true holiness
in the Christian, or a life in the power of Christ's love.

* * *

5 To be a Christian just means to have the Spirit of Christ,
to have His love, and to have been made by Him a fountain of love, springing up and flowing out in streams of living
water. We know not what the Spirit is meant to be in us,
because we have not accepted Him for what the Master gave.

* * *

6 It is only where the soul gives the Spirit the precedence
it claims, and self is denied to make way for God, that
selfishness will be conquered, and love toward our brother
flow from love toward God.

7 Not the amount, or the clearness, or the interest of the
Bible knowledge received will decide the blessing and
the power that it brings, but the measure of real dependence
on the Holy Spirit.

* * *

8 It is not the power of intellect, it is not even the earnest
desire to know the truth, that fits a man for the Spirit's
teaching; it is a life yielded to Him in waiting dependence
and full obedience to be made spiritual, that receives the
spiritual wisdom and understanding.

* * *

9 Believe! It is not enough that the light of Christ shines
on you in the Word — the light of the Spirit must shine
in you.

* * *

10 It is the very work of the Spirit specially to unite Himself with what is material, to lift it up into His own Spirit
nature, and so to develop what will be the highest type of
perfection — a spiritual body.

* * *

11 In the Father we have the unseen God, the Author of
all. In the Son, God revealed and brought nigh. In
the Spirit of God we have the indwelling God, the power of
God dwelling in human body and working in it what the
Father and the Son have for us.

* * *

12 As all the Word of God is given by the Spirit of God,
so each word must be interpreted to us by that same
Spirit. Not in the Spirit without or with but little of the Word,
not in the Word without or with but little of the Spirit, but
in the Word and Spirit, both dwelling richly within us, and
both yielded to in implicit obedience, is our assurance of
safety in the path of the Spirit's guidance.

13 The Holy Spirit is the Church's power for all her work and her missions, and that power will only act mightily as the number increases of individual believers, who give themselves to be possessed, to be led, to be used of the Spirit of Christ.

* * *

14 When the Holy Spirit convinces us of the sin of the world, His work bears two marks. The one is the sacrifice of self in the jealousy for God and His honour, combined with the deep and tender grief for the guilty. The other is a deep, strong faith in the possibility and power of deliverance.

* * *

15 God looks upon the world in His holiness, hating its sin with such an infinite hatred, and loving it with such a love that He gives His Son, and the Son gives His life to destroy sin and set its captives free.

Not in what *we know,* but in what *we are* does the Spirit begin His work. And the teaching of the Spirit begins not in word or thought, but in power.

* * *

16 There is no way of knowing the light but by being in it and using it. There is no way of knowing the Holy Spirit but by possessing Him and being possessed of Him. To have Him in us, doing His work and giving us His fellowship, this is the path the Master opens when He says, "Ye know Him, for He shall be in you."

* * *

17 However little we see or feel, let us believe. The Divine is always first known by believing. As we continue believing, we shall be prepared to know and to see.

Gather together all the Word says of the Spirit, His indwelling and His work, and hide it in your heart. Be determined to accept of nothing but what the Word teaches, but also to accept heartily of all it teaches.

18 God is to be found nowhere but in His will. His will
       in Christ accepted, and done by us, with the heart in
which it is done, is the home of the Holy Spirit.

Even now, day by day, we are to live in His glory. The
Holy Spirit is able to be to us just as much as we are willing
to have of Him and of the life of the glorified Lord.

*   *   *

19 Let us come under the hand of our Lord, covered by
       His hand with only one purpose — to have all our work
covered in the hand of our Lord. *There* is the secret of life.

The Holy Ghost never looked for His own glory, never
spoke of His own: His only purpose is to glorify Christ. It
was not obligation but the yearning of His heart, this de-
crease.

*   *   *

20 Learn to look on Jesus, and more and more you will
       find that Jesus by His look is taking your wandering
look under the direction of the Holy Ghost. By and by it
will become the very attitude of your soul, and you could do
anything more easily than distrust Jesus.

Behind the Valley of Death there is abundance of life, and
the moment you give up all things, letting yourself go in the
arms of Jesus, death will lose its terror.

*   *   *

21 If you want unity in your daily life, don't seek life;
       never will you find life if you are seeking for it. Life
is only when you have your own life.

I am too happy not to put every day, every hour in the
hands of my Heavenly Father; too happy ever again to take
into my hand the threads of my life.

*   *   *

22 A seed contains life hidden in the most dead, unlikely
       looking form possible, and this seed, with its hidden
life, must itself again be hidden under the earth. So the kingdom of heaven comes to us in the seed of the Word. It must

41

be hidden not in the thoughts that we can recognise and watch over, but deeper down, in the mysterious depths of the spirit. There Christ, who is in the unseen Spirit life of the Father, finds the unseen depths of our spirit life and enters there. He is Himself the Living Word, the Living Seed; the Spirit is the life of the seed.

* * *

23 It is often only as we suffer in the flesh that the quickening of the Spirit is experienced. All leading claims following, it is easily understood that to enjoy the leading of the Spirit demands a very teachable, followsome mind.

Even as beautiful flames on earth are nothing but the wood or coal transformed by the fire into its own light nature, so the fire of God cleanses and beautifies by filling the heart with its own heavenly glory. (Miscellaneous.)

In all our life process we must be made like unto Him. He received His life from God; He lived it in dependence upon God; He gave up His life to God; He was raised from the dead by God; He lives His life in glory with God. (Miscellaneous.)

* * *

24 What a blessed solution God gives to all our questions and our difficulties when He says, "My child, Christ has gone through it all for thee!" He has wrought out a new nature that can trust God, and Christ the Living One in heaven will live in thee, and enable thee to live that life of trust (Miscellaneous.)

* * *

25 Just as much as Christ was my Substitute who died for me, just so much He is my Head in whom and with whom I die. Just as He lives for me to intercede, He lives in me to carry out and perfect His life. By His death He proved that He possessed life only to hold it, and to spend it, for God. (Miscellaneous.)

26   Ask God to make you willing to believe with your heart
that to die with Christ is the only way to live in Him.
Jesus lived every day in the prospect of the Cross, and we
in the power of His victorious life, being made conformable
to His death, must rejoice every day in going down with Him
into death. (Miscellaneous.)

*   *   *

27   The acorn died and the tree appeared. In the very
grave, where the acorn died, it stood there stretching
its roots deeper and deeper into the earth, yet growing higher,
stronger, broader, more beautiful. All the fruit and all the
foliage it owes to that grave in which its roots are cast and
kept. Even so, Christ owes everything to His grave, and we,
too, owe everything to the grave of Jesus. (Miscellaneous.)

*   *   *

28   Christ lost nothing by giving up His life unto the Father.
If you want the glory and the life of God to come upon
you, it is in the grave of utter helplessness that that life of
glory will be born. (Miscellaneous.)

The secret of being in nothing behind the chiefest apostles
— in nothing behind even Paul himself — is this: "I am nothing!" Why? "Because God hath chosen the things that are
not." Why? "That no flesh should glory in His presence,
he that glorieth, let him glory in the Lord." To be nothing
is the only way to let God be all. (Miscellaneous.)

*   *   *

29   Jesus came to deliver man from sin and sickness, that
He might make known the love of the Father. In His
actions, in the teaching of the disciples, in the work of the
Holy Spirit, and in the words of the apostles, pardon and
healing are always to be found together. To receive healing,
it is necessary to begin by confession of sin and the purpose
to live a holy life. This is why those who receive healing
receive at the same time new spiritual blessing, feel more
closely united to the Lord Jesus, and learn to love and serve

43

Him better. The redeemed may always cry, "Bless the Lord, O my soul, who forgiveth all thine iniquities, who healeth all thy diseases." (Ps. 103:3.) (Miscellaneous.)

* * *

30 The preaching of the gospel and the healing of the sick are given as evident proof of Christ's mission as the Messiah. (Matt. 11:5.) Jesus, who took upon Him the soul and body of man, delivers both in equal measure from the consequences of sin. When Christ speaks of sickness, it is always as of an evil caused by sin and Satan. He declared that every disciple would have to bear his cross. (Matt. 16: 24.) But He never taught one sick person to resign himself to be sick. Sin in the soul and sickness in the body, both bear witness to the power of Satan; and "The Son of Man was manifested that He might destroy the works of the devil." (I John 3:8; Job 2:7; Luke 13:16; Acts 10:38; Heb. 2:14; Gen. 1:31.) (Miscellaneous.)

1 In our blessed Priest-King, Jesus Christ, the kingly power
is founded on the priestly, "He is able to save to the
uttermost, because He ever liveth to make intercession." In
us, His priests and kings, it is no otherwise.

As long as we look on prayer chiefly as the means of maintaining our own Christian life, we shall not know fully what
it is meant to be.

Jesus never taught His disciples how to preach, only how
to pray. To know how to speak to God is more than knowing how to speak to man. Not power with men, but power
with God is the first thing. Do not be thinking of how little
you have to bring God, but of how much He wants to give
you.

*   *   *

2 Not on the strong or the fervent feeling with which I
pray does the blessing depend, but upon the love and
the power of the Father to whom I intrust my needs.

The knowledge of God's Father-love is the first and sim-
plest, but also the last and highest lesson in the school of
prayer. The sooner I learn to forget myself in the desire that
He may be glorified, the richer will the blessing be that prayer
will bring to myself. No one ever loses by what he sacrifices
for the Father.

*   *   *

3 Because the will of God is the glory of heaven, the doing
of it is the blessedness of heaven. As the will is done,
the kingdom of heaven comes into the heart, and wherever
faith has accepted the Father's will. The surrender to, and
the prayer for a life of heaven-like obedience, is the spirit
of childlike prayer.

As a child has to prove a sum to be correct, so the proof
that we have prayed aright is the answer. In prayer and its
answer the interchange of love between the Father and His
child takes place. Man's prayer on earth and God's answer

45

in heaven are meant for each other. A life marked by daily answer to prayer is the proof of our spiritual maturity.

*   *   *

4   If the child is to know and understand his father; if, as he grows up, he is to enter into all his will and plans; if he is to have his highest joy in the father, and the father in him, he must be of one mind and spirit with him. And so it is impossible to conceive of God bestowing any higher gift on His child than this, His own Spirit. God is what He is through His Spirit; the Spirit is the very life of God.

It is when we give ourselves to be a blessing that we can especially count on the blessings of God. The righteous man who is the friend of the poor is very specially the friend of God. This gives wonderful liberty in prayer. Every believer is a labourer; not one of God's children who has not been redeemed for service, and has not his work waiting.

*   *   *

5   As long as in prayer we just pour out our hearts in a multitude of petitions without taking time to see whether every petition is sent with the purpose and expectation of getting an answer, not many will reach the mark.

It is when in distinct matters we have in faith claimed and received answers that our more general prayers will be believing and effectual.

As we think how all He is and has, how He Himself is our life, we feel assured that we have but to ask, and He will be delighted to take us up into closer fellowship with Himself, and teach us to pray even as He prays. A life in God's infinite Fatherliness and continual answers to prayer are inseparable, but the child who only wants to know the love of the Father when he has something to ask will be disappointed.

Faith is nothing but the purpose of the will resting on God's word, and saying, "I must have it." To believe truly, is to will firmly.

6 Believe that you have received now, while praying, the thing you ask for. It may only be later that you shall see what you believe; but now, without seeing, you are to believe that it has been given you of the Father in heaven.

Faith says most confidently, "I have received the promise." Patience perseveres in prayer until the gift bestowed in heaven is seen on earth. Believe that ye have received, and ye shall have!

Between the "have received" in heaven, and the "shall have" on earth, believe; believing praise and prayer is the link.

* * *

7 Let faith look to God more than the thing promised. The cure of a feeble faith is alone to be found in the invigoration of our whole spiritual life by intercourse with God. Learn to believe in God, to take hold of God, to let God take possession of thy life, and it will be easy to take hold of the promise. He that knows and trusts God finds it easy to trust the promise too.

* * *

8 Men of strong faith are men of much prayer. It is in the dying to self which much prayer implies, in closer union to Jesus, that the spirit of faith will come in power. Faith needs prayer for its full growth.

It is only in a life of temperance and self-denial that there will be the heart or the strength to pray much.

Without voluntary separation even from what is lawful, no one will attain power in prayer.

* * *

9 Not according to what I try to be when praying, but what I am when not praying, is my prayer dealt with by God.

Nothing would be more unnatural than that the children of a family should always meet their father separately, but never in the united expression of their desires or their love. It is in the union and fellowship of believers that the Spirit can manifest His full power.

*   *   *

10 Man in his spiritual nature is under the law of gradual growth that reigns in all created life. It is only in the path of development that he can reach his Divine destiny. The Father alone knows the moment when the soul or the Church is ripened to that fulness of faith in which it can really take and keep the blessing. As a father who longs to have his only child home from school, and yet waits patiently till the time of training is completed, so it is with God and His children. He is the Longsuffering One, and answers speedily.

*   *   *

11 Prayer not only teaches and strengthens to work: work teaches and strengthens to pray. Faith is obedience at home and looking to the Master: obedience is faith going out to do His will.

As a Christian grows in grace and in knowledge of the Lord Jesus, he is often surprised to find how the words of God grow too, in the new and deeper meaning with which they come to him.

Just as far as we listen to the voice and language that God speaks, and in the words of God, receive His thoughts, His mind, His life, into our heart, we shall learn to speak in the voice and language that God hears.

*   *   *

12 The Old Testament saints spake in prayer. If the word was a command, they simply did as the Lord had spoken: their life was fellowship with God, the interchange of word and thought. What God spoke they heard and did; what they spoke God heard and did.

Let us believe that we can know if our prayer be accord-

ing to God's will. Let us yield our heart to have the word
of the Father dwell richly there. Let us live day by day with
the anointing which teacheth all things, and we shall soon
understand how the Father's love longs that the child should
know His will, and should, in the confidence that that will
includes all that His power and love have promised to do,
know too that He hears the petitions which we ask of Him.

*   *   *

13 God wills a great deal of blessing to His people, which
never comes to them. He wills it most earnestly, but
they do not will it, and it cannot come to them.

Our true aim must not be to work much, but to pray
much, and then to work enough for the power and blessing
obtained in prayer to find its way through us to men.

Because we do not abide in Christ as He would have us,
the Church is so impotent in presence of the infidelity and
worldliness and heathendom, in the midst of which the Lord
is able to make her more than conqueror. Let us believe
that He means what He promises, and accept the condemnation the confession implies.

THE MINISTRY OF INTERCESSION

14 The measure of believing, continued prayer, will be
the measure of the Spirit's working in the Church.
Direct, definite, determined prayer is what we need. The
measure of God's giving the Spirit, is our asking. He gives
as a father to him who asks as a child.

There is nothing in honest business, when it is kept in its
place as entirely subordinate to the kingdom, which must
ever be first, that need prevent fellowship with God.

*   *   *

15 A much-praying minister will receive an entrance into
God's will he would otherwise know nothing of; will
be brought to praying people where he does not expect them;
will receive blessing above all he asks or thinks. It is prayer

that is the only secret of true Church extension; that is guided from heaven to find and set forth God-called and God-empowered men.

The attempt to pray constantly for ourselves must be a failure; it is in intercession for others that our faith and love and perseverance will be aroused, and that the power of the Spirit be found, which can fit us for saving men.

* * *

16 Intercession is the most perfect form of prayer: it is the prayer Christ ever liveth to pray on His throne.

It is as love of our profession and work, delight in thoroughness and diligence, sink away in the tender compassion of Christ, that love will compel us to prayer, because we cannot rest in our work if souls are not saved. True love must pray.

Just as the heaven our natural eye can see is one great ocean of sunshine, with its light and heat-giving beauty and fruitfulness to earth, Scripture shows us God's true heaven, filled with all spiritual blessings, Divine light and love and life, heavenly joy and peace and power, all shining down upon us.

* * *

17 If we will but believe in God and His faithfulness, intercession will become to us the very first thing we take refuge in when we seek blessing for others, and the very last thing for which we cannot find time.

Prayer opens the way for God Himself to do His work in us and through us. Let our chief work, as God's messengers, be intercession: in it we secure the presence and power of God to go with us.

Let us confess before God our lack of prayer. Let us admit that the lack of faith, of which it is the proof, is the symptom of a life that is not spiritual, that is yet all too much under the power of self and the flesh and the world.

18 In all ages men have prayed under a sense that there
were difficulties in the heavenly world to overcome.
As they pleaded with God, and in that persevering supplication were brought into union with His will, and of faith that
could take hold of Him, the hindrances in themselves and in
heaven were together overcome. As God conquered them,
they conquered God. As God prevails over us, we prevail
with God.

Faith in a prayer-hearing God will make a prayer-loving
Christian.

Where our life is right, we shall know how to pray so as
to please God, and prayer will secure the answer.

The man who is ready to risk all for God can count upon
God to do all for him. It is as men live that they pray. It
is the life that prays.

* * *

19 The more we pray, and the more conscious we become
of our unfitness to pray in power, the more we shall be
urged and helped to press on toward the secret of power in
prayer — a life abiding in Christ, entirely at His disposal.
This marks off the wholehearted believer from the worldling
and worldly Christians around him; he lives consciously hidden in the secret of God's presence.

When the pressure of work for Christ is allowed to be the
excuse for our not finding time to seek and secure His own
presence and power in it, as our chief need, it surely proves
that there is no right sense of our absolute dependence upon
God, no true entrance into the heavenly, altogether other-
worldly character of our incision and aims, no full surrender
to and delight in Jesus Christ Himself.

* * *

20 When once we see how there is to be nothing of our
own for a single moment, and that it is to be all Christ,
moment by moment, and learn to accept it from Him, and
trust Him for it, the life of Christ becomes the health of our

soul. Health is nothing but life in its normal, undisturbed action. Christ gives us health by giving us Himself as our life; so He becomes our strength for our walk. They that wait on the Lord shall walk and not faint, because Christ is now the strength of their life.

* * *

21 The more heartily we enter into the mind of our blessed Lord, and set ourselves simply just to think about prayer as He thought, the more surely will His words be as living seeds. They will grow and produce in us their fruit — a life and practice exactly corresponding to the Divine truth they contain.

A Christian may often have very earnest desires for spiritual blessings. But alongside of these there are other desires in his daily life, occupying a large place in his interests and affections. The spiritual desires are not all-absorbing. He wonders that his prayer is not heard. It is simply that God wants the whole heart. "The Lord thy God is one Lord, therefore thou shalt love the Lord thy God with thy whole heart."

* * *

22 Prayer is just the breathing of the Spirit in us; power in prayer comes from the power of the Spirit in us, waited on and trusted in. Failure in prayer comes from feebleness of the Spirit's work in us. To pray aright, the life of the Spirit must be right in us.

As long as we measure our power for praying aright and perseveringly, by what we feel or think we can accomplish, we shall be discouraged when we hear of how much we ought to pray. But when we quietly believe that, in the midst of all our conscious weakness, the Holy Spirit, as a Spirit of Supplication, is dwelling within us for the very purpose of enabling us to pray in such manner and measure as God would have us, our hearts will be filled with hope.

23 The Spirit can pray in no other way in us than as He lives in us. It is only as we give ourselves to the Spirit living and praying in us that the glory of the prayer-hearing God and the ever-blessed and most effectual mediation of the Son can be known by us in their power.

When we realise what time Christ spent in prayer, and how the great events of His life were all connected with special prayer, we learn the necessity of absolute dependence on and unceasing direct communication with the heavenly world, if we are to live a heavenly life, or to exercise heavenly power around us.

* * *

24 If anyone could have been satisfied with always living and working in the spirit of prayer, it would have been our Master. But He could not; He needed to have His supplies replenished by continual and long-continued seasons of prayer.

Christ was what He taught. All His teaching was just the revelation of how He lived, and — praise God — of the life He was to lead in us.

Even as Christ obtained His right of prevailing intercession by His giving Himself a sacrifice to God for men, and through it receives the blessings He dispenses; so, if we have truly with Christ given ourselves to God for men, we share His right of intercession, and are able to obtain the powers of the heavenly world for them too.

* * *

25 Tell everyone who is master of his own time that he is as the angels, free to tarry before the throne, and then go out and minister to the heirs of salvation.

We are frequently in danger of looking to what God has done and is doing, and to count on that as the pledge that He will at once do more. And all the time it may be true that He is blessing us up to the measure of our faith or self-sacrifice, and cannot give larger measure until there has been a new discovery and confession of what is hindering Him.

* * *

26 Men would fain have a revival as the outgrowth of their agencies and progress. God's way is the opposite: it is out of death, acknowledged as the desert of sin, confessed as utter helplessness, that He revives. He revives the heart of the contrite one.

When earnest, godly workers allow, against their better will, the spiritual to be crowded out by incessant occupation and the fatigue it brings, it must be because the spiritual life is not sufficiently strong in them to bid the lever stand aside till the presence of God in Christ and the power of the Spirit have been fully secured.

* * *

27 It was when the friend at midnight, in answer to his prayer, had received from another as much as he needed, that he could supply his hungry friend. It was the intercession, going out and importuning, that was the difficult work; returning home with his rich supply to impart was easy, joyful work. This is Christ's divine order for all thy work, my brother: First come in utter poverty, every day, and get from God the blessing in intercession; go then rejoicingly to impart it.

* * *

28 Our Lord gave His disciples on His resurrection day the Holy Spirit, to enable them to wait for the full outpouring on the day of Pentecost. It is only in the power of the Spirit already in us, acknowledged and yielded to, that we can pray for His fuller manifestation. Say to the Father, it is the Spirit of His Son in you is urging you to plead His promise.

Prayer is not only wishing or asking, but believing and accepting.

29 In the last night Christ asked three things for His disciples: that they might be kept as those who are not of the world; that they might be sanctified; that they might be one in love. You cannot do better than pray as Jesus prayed. Ask for God's people that they may be kept separate from the world and its spirit; that they, by the Holy Spirit, may live as those who are not of the world.

The utterance of our wish gives point to the transaction in which we are engaged with God, and so awakens faith and expectation. Be very definite in your petitions, so as to know what answer you may look for.

* * *

30 The future of the Church and world depends, to an extent we little conceive, on the education of the day. The Church may be seeking to evangelise the heathen and be giving up her own children to secular and materialistic influences. Pray for schools and colleges, and that the Church may realise and fulfil its momentous duty of caring for its children.

Beware in your prayer, above everything, of limiting God, not only by unbelief, but by fancying that you know what He can do. Expect unexpected things, above all that we ask or think. Each time that you intercede, be quiet first and worship God in His glory.

The same censer brings the prayer of the saints before God, and casts fire upon the earth. The prayers that go up to heaven have their share in the history of this earth.

* * *

31 Pray for the Jews. Their return to the God of their fathers stands connected, in a way we cannot tell, with wonderful blessing to the Church, and with the coming of our Lord Jesus.

What numbers of Bibles are being circulated. What numbers of sermons on the Bible are being preached. What numbers of Bibles being read in home and school. How little blessing when it comes "in word" only; what Divine blessing and power when it comes "in the Holy Ghost," when it is preached "with the Holy Ghost sent forth from heaven."

All the powers of evil seek to hinder us in prayer. Prayer is a conflict with opposing forces. It needs the whole heart and all our strength. May God give us grace to strive in prayer until we prevail.

1 The benefit of meetings for bringing and reading aloud
   texts on a point previously announced is very great. This
practice leads to the searching of God's Word, as even preaching does not.

* * *

2 Read a book to understand the good, and then see if you
   receive benefit from the thoughts expressed. Read to
see if it is really in accordance with God's Word. Read to
find out the corresponding places, not in the Bible, but in
your own life. Know if your life has been in harmony with
the new life; direct your life for the future entirely according
to God's Word.

* * *

3 One verse chosen to meet your needs, read ten times
   and then laid up in the heart, is better than ten verses
read once. Only so much of the Word as I actually receive
and inwardly appropriate for myself is food for my soul.

* * *

4 With God, speaking and doing always go together: "Shall
   He say it and not do it?" The deed follows the word. I
hear what God has said. I take time to lodge in my heart the
word promised: I await the fulfilment. God promises — I believe — God fulfils: that is the secret of the new life.

* * *

5 The Christian has only to believe; God will look to the
   fulfilling. He thinks that he must have a great power to
exercise such a great faith. You must not bring this mighty
faith to get the Word fulfilled; the Word brings you this faith.
"The Word is living and powerful." "Faith is by the Word."
Keep yourselves occupied with the Word and give it time.
It will work in you a faith strong and able for anything.

* * *

6 If I trust in the Word, and in the living God, His commandment will work in me desire and power for obedience. When I weigh and hold fast the command, it works the

desire and the will to obey; it urges strongly the conviction that I can certainly do what my Father says. The Word, as the command of the living God who loves me, is my power.

* * *

7 This is the love of God; not that He gives us something, but someone — a living person — not one or another blessing, but Him in whom is all life and blessing, — Jesus Himself. The whole of salvation consists in this: to have, to enjoy, Jesus. "He that hath the Son hath life."

* * *

8 God gives in a wonderful way: from the heart, completely for nothing, to the unworthy. And He gives effectually. What He gives He will really make entirely our possession. To take Jesus, and to hold Him fast and use Him when received, is our great work. And that taking is nothing but trusting. He is mine, with all that He has.

* * *

9 It was in His great love that the Father gave the Son. It was out of love that Jesus gave Himself. The taking, the having of Jesus, is the entrance to a life in the love of God: this is the highest life. Through faith we must press into love, and dwell there.

* * *

10 Keep back no single sin. Keep back no single power. To save is to free from sin. Wait not till you enter into temptation, but let your life beforehand be always through Jesus.

* * *

11 The continued indeterminate confession of sin does more harm than good. It is much better to say to God that you have nothing to confess, than to confess you know not what.

* * *

12 The secret of progress in the service of God is a strong yearning to become free from every sin, a hunger and

thirst after righteousness. The Spirit of God is named the Holy Spirit, because He makes us holy. Being right with God is followed by doing right.

* * *

13   You must love, although you do not feel the least love.
It is not in your feeling, but in faith, that the Spirit in you is the power of your will to work in you all that the Father bids you. Therefore, although you feel absolutely no love to your enemy, say, "In faith, in the hidden working of the Spirit in my heart, I do love him."

* * *

14   The nearer we are to God, the less we are in ourselves, but the stronger we are in Him. The more I see of God, the less I become, the deeper is my confidence in Him. To become lowly, let God fill eye and heart. Where God is all, there is no time or place for man.

* * *

15   You often pray and strive against a sin: although this is done with God's help you would be the person who would overcome. No! "the battle is not yours, but God's." Ask only, "What is my Jesus able to do?" What you really trust Him with, He is able to keep. You can trust the power of Jesus, if you know that He is yours, if you hold converse with Him as your friend.

* * *

16   "The Lord must help me to overcome sin:" the expression is altogether outside of the New Testament. The grace of God in the soul does not become a help to us. He will do everything. When you surrender anything to the Lord for keeping, take heed that you give it wholly into His hands, and that you leave it there. He will carry out your case gloriously.

* * *

17   The complaint about weakness is often nothing else than an apology for our idleness. There is power to be obtained in Christ for those who will take the pains to have it. Strength is for work. He who would be strong simply to be pious will not be so. He who in his weakness begins to work for the Lord shall become strong.

* * *

18 Believing right in opposition to what we see gives salvation. The unbelief that would see shall not see; the faith that will not see, but has enough in God, shall see the glory of God. Feeling always seeks something in itself; faith keeps itself occupied with what Jesus is.

* * *

19 Our work every day and the whole day is to believe. Out of faith come all blessings and powers, also the victory for overcoming. The blessing of God includes in it the power of life for multiplication, for expansion, for communication. In the Scriptures blessing and multiplication go together. Blessing always includes the power to bless others.

* * *

20 For missions Jesus left the throne of heaven. The heathen are His inheritance. In heathendom the power of Satan has been established. Jesus must have Himself vindicated as the conqueror. The Lord has made Himself dependent upon His body to do His work. It is the work for which the Holy Spirit was given. See this in the leading of the Spirit vouchsafed to Peter and Barnabas and Saul. Missionary work brings blessing on the Church. It rouses to heroic deeds of faith and self-denial. It has furnished the most glorious instances of the wondrous power of the Lord. In love for missionary work you will learn to cleave to God and the Word; you will be drawn into prayer.

* * *

21 Gladness in God is the strongest proof that I have in God what satisfies me. Gladness is the token of the truth and the worth of obedience, showing I have pleasure in the will of God. The light of God's countenance gives the

Christian his gladness: in fellowship with his Lord he always
will be happy: the love of the Father shines like the sun
upon His children. Sin makes dark; unbelief also makes
dark, for it turns us from Him who alone is the light.

* * *

22 Gladness is hindered by ignorance, when we do not understand God and His love and the blessedness of His
service; by double-heartedness, when we are not willing to
give up everything for Jesus.

* * *

23 Do not seek gladness; in that case you will not find it,
because you are seeking feeling. But seek Jesus, follow
Jesus, believe in Jesus, and gladness shall be added to you.

* * *

24 The will of God is as perfect as He Himself: let us not
be afraid to surrender ourselves to it: no one suffers
loss by deeming the will of God unconditionally good.

The sure confidence of an answer is the secret of powerful
praying. For a blessed prayer-meeting there must be love
and unity among the suppliants, agreement upon the definite
object that is desired; the coming together in the name of
Jesus, and the consciousness of His presence. According to
your conviction of the nearness of God will be the power of
your prayer.

* * *

25 When the Lord Jesus manifests His great grace to a
soul in redeeming it, He desires that the world should
see and know it: He would be known and honoured as its
proprietor. Apart from this public confession surrender is
but half-hearted.

* * *

26 Conformity to the world can be overcome by nothing
but conformity to Jesus. Conformity to the world is
strengthened especially by intercourse with it: it is in intercourse with Jesus that we shall adopt His mode of thinking,

His disposition, His manners. This is the spirit of the world: to seek one's self and the visible. The Spirit of Jesus: to live for God and the things that are invisible.

*   *   *

27 Do not use the day of rest only as a day for the public observance of Divine worship. In the Church you have the ordinances of preaching, united prayer and praise, to keep you occupied. It is especially in private personal intercourse that God can bless and sanctify you.

*   *   *

28 The lessons of the Supper are many. It is a feast of remembrance, a feast of reconciliation, a covenant feast, a feast of hope. But all these separate thoughts are only subordinate parts of the principal element: the living Jesus would give Himself to us in the most inward union.

*   *   *

29 There is but one Hebrew word for "obeying voice" and "hearing voice": when I learn the will of God, not in the words of a man or a book, but from God Himself, I shall surely believe what is promised and do what is commanded. The Holy Spirit is the voice of God: when we hear the living voice obedience becomes easy.

*   *   *

30 Read the Word with a searching of the Scriptures. The best explanation of the Bible is the Bible itself. Take three or four texts upon a point and compare them. See wherein they agree and wherein they differ; where they say the same thing or again something else. Let the Word of God be cleared up and confirmed by what He said at another time on the same subject. The sacred writers use this method of instruction with the Scriptures.

1 The secret of the life of holiness comes to those who seek it not, but only seek Jesus. Let all learn to trust in Jesus and to rejoice in Him, even though their experience be not what they would wish. He will make us holy. But whether we have entered the blessed life of faith in Jesus as our sanctification, or are still longing for it from afar, we all need one thing — the simple believing and obedient acceptance of each word that our God has spoken.

*   *   *

2 "Be ye holy, for I am holy." It is as if God said: Holiness is My blessedness and My glory; without this you cannot see Me or enjoy Me. There is nothing higher to be conceived; I invite you to share with Me in it; I invite you to likeness with Myself: "Be ye holy, for I am holy."

*   *   *

3 Holiness is not something we do or attain; it is the communication of the Divine Life, the inbreathing of the Divine Nature; the power of the Divine Presence resting on us. The Holy One calls us to Himself, that He may make us holy in possessing Himself. It is because the call to holiness comes from the God of infinite Power and Love that we may have the confidence: we can be holy.

*   *   *

4 The nature of light is the same, whether in the sun or in a candle; the nature of holiness remains unchanged whether it be God or man in whom it dwells. The more carefully we listen to God's voice and let it sink into our hearts, the more will all human standards fall away, and only the words be heard, "Holy, as I am holy."

*   *   *

5 We are holy in Christ Jesus. Would we but believe, how God's light would shine and fill our hearts with joy and love. Let us fear our own thoughts and crucify our own wisdom. Let us give ourselves up to receive, in the power of the life of God Himself, working in us by the Holy Spirit, that which is deeper and truer than human thought, Christ Himself as our holiness.

* * *

6 As the revelation of the Holy One of old was a very slow and gradual one, so let us be content patiently to follow, step by step, the path of the shining light through the Word; it will shine more and more unto the perfect day.

* * *

7 All God's teaching about holiness is comprised in three great lessons: — First, a revelation, "I am holy"; second, a command, "Be ye holy"; third, a gift, the link between the two, "Ye are holy in Christ."

* * *

8 It is the consciousness of God's presence, making and keeping us His very own, that works the true separateness of the world and its spirit from ourselves and our will. It is as this separation is prized and persevered in that the holiness of God will enter in and take possession.

* * *

9 Because God is a spiritual and invisible Being, every revelation of Himself, whether in His work, His Word, or His Son, calls for faith. Faith is to the soul what the senses are to the body; by it alone we enter into communication and contact with God. Faith is that meekness of soul which waits in stillness to hear, to understand, to accept what God says, to receive, to retain, to possess what God gives. By faith we allow God to become our very life. And because holiness is God's highest glory and blessing, it is especially in the life of holiness that we need to live by faith alone.

* * *

10 True holiness, God's holiness, in us works itself out in love, in seeking and loving the unholy that they may become holy too. Self-sacrificing love is of the very essence of holiness.

11 The will of God must first live in us, if it is to be done by us. The way for us to have God's power in us is for ourselves to be in His power. Put yourself into the power of God; let the Holy Spirit dwell within as in His Holy Temple, revealing the Holy One on the throne; ruling all. Holiness is essential to effectual service.

*   *   *

12 If in our study of the way of holiness there has been awakened in us the desire to accept and adore and stand complete in all the will of God, let us seek to recognise that will in everything that comes on us. The sin of him who vexes us is not God's will. But it is God's will that we should be in that position of difficulty to be tried and tested. Such acceptance of the trial turns it into a blessing. It will lead on to an ever clearer abiding in all the will of God all the day.

*   *   *

13 The more deeply we enter by faith into our liberty which we have in Christ, the more joyfully and confidently we present our members to God as instruments of righteousness. The liberty is not lawlessness: "We are delivered from our enemies that we may serve Him in righteousness and holiness all the days of our life."

*   *   *

14 The secret of true holiness is a very direct and personal relation to the Holy One; all the teaching through the Word or men made entirely dependent on, and subordinate to the personal teaching of the Holy Ghost.

*   *   *

15 How many weary workers there are mourning the want of power. They have spent their strength more in the outer court of work and service than in the inner life of fellowship and faith.

LOVE MADE PERFECT

16 To think that that everlasting God who created heaven
and earth should deal with each one of us individually,
and that it should please Him to fill *us* with that everlasting
love in which the Father begot the Son and in which the
Holy Spirit maintains the fellowship between Father and Son.

* * *

17 I must not seek for love, but for God, for love is the
very nature of God. It does not say God *has* love, but
God *is* love, and the love that I need is God Himself coming
into my heart.

When the soul is perfected in love, it has such a sense of
that love that it can rest in it for eternity, and though it has
as much as it can contain for the time being, it can always
receive more.

* * *

18 If we loved others with the love of God, how much
more power there would be in our work, how much
more intercession, how much we should sacrifice everything,
our formality, our habits. We would do work breathed upon
by the love of God.

* * *

19 It is only the love of God coming in that will cast out
self; but self must be brought as a criminal to His feet.
When God brings a man to see all that there is in Christ, and
to receive Christ fully, the power of Christ's death can come
upon him and he can die to sin, and if he dies to sin, he dies
to self.

* * *

20 The work of God the Father is to beget God the Son,
and that is the work which goes on through eternity.
God has nothing for us but Jesus, but He is willing to give
this — the living Son, born afresh into us. When the living
Christ dwells in us, He will break open the fountain of love
within us.

21 Love means giving, and giving all. God gave His Son to me, and with Him gave all; and now, love is — God claiming everything.

In the light of Christ's love, perfect love means that we give up ourselves to pray and to work for others.

The love and the faith of Christ's disciples was very defective, yet Christ accepted it as the obedience and the faith of loving hearts. So, if we come to Christ with our feeble beginnings, He will receive our love, and will day by day lead us in the path of perfect love and of perfect obedience.

Just as we must be separate from the world and joined to Christ in obedience to His Word, so we must also be joined to each other.

* * *

BE PERFECT

22 A child may be the perfect image of his father. There may be a great difference in power and yet the resemblance may be so striking that everyone notices it; so a child of God, though infinitely less, may yet bear the image of the Father so markedly that in his creaturely life he shall be perfect as the Father is in His divine life.

Man was created simply to show forth God's glory, by allowing God to show how completely He could reveal His likeness and blessedness in man.

A life that is wholly for God has in all ages been accepted by the Father as the mark of the perfect man.

* * *

23 The work of the child is very defective and yet cause of joy and hope to the father, because he sees in it proof of the child's attachment and obedience, as well as the pledge of what that spirit will do for the child when his intelligence and his strength have been increased. The child has served the father with a perfect heart, though the perfect heart does not at once imply perfect work.

24 If we are to have perfect peace and confidence, we must know that our heart is perfect with God. The consciousness of a perfect heart gives wonderful power in prayer.

It is just he who knows most of what it is to be perfect in purpose who will pray most to be perfect in practice too. Walking before God will ensure walking in His commandments.

Faith expects from God what is beyond all expectation.

* * *

25 To have God reveal His strength in us, to have Him make us strong for life or work, for doing or for suffering, our heart must be perfect with Him.

God is Love, who lives not for Himself, but in the energy of an infinite life makes His creatures, as far as they can possibly receive it, partakers of His perfection.

As little as there can be a ray of the light of day, however dull and clouded it be, but what speaks of the sun, so little can there be any perfection but what is of God.

* * *

26 A man may have his heart intent on serving God perfectly, and yet he may be unconscious of how very imperfect his knowledge of God's will is. The soul that longs to be perfect in the way, and in deep consciousness of its need of a Divine teaching pleads for it, will not be disappointed.

* * *

27 "Let us go on to perfection" means, let us go on to know Christ perfectly, to live entirely by His heavenly life now He is perfected, to follow wholly His earthly life and the path in which He reached perfection.

There must be harmony between the place of worship and the worshippers. As He has prepared the perfect sanctuary, the Holiest of All, for us, He has prepared us for it too.

On our part, the surrender to be made perfect will be the measure of our capacity to apprehend what God has done in Christ.

28　A valuable piece of machinery may be out of order. The owner has spent time and trouble in vain to put it right. The maker comes: it costs him but a moment to remove the hindrance. So the soul that has for years wearied itself in the effort to do God's will may often in one moment be delivered from some misapprehension as to what God demands or promises, find itself restored, perfected for every good thing. What was done in a moment becomes the secret of the continuous life, as faith each day claims the God that perfects, to do that which is well-pleasing in His sight.

*　　*　　*

29　Jesus Christ was Himself not perfected in one day; in Him patience had its perfect work. True faith recognises the need of time, and rests in God.

The weakest point in the character of the Christian is the measure of His nearness to perfection. It is in the little things of daily life that perfection is attained and proved.

*　　*　　*

30　There is the inward perfection that comes from growth and development, and the perfection which consists in having defects removed and what is lacking supplied. Only the former could be used of the Lord Jesus, not the latter. Both have reference to what God seeks in His children and works in them.

No one will pray for the perfected heart earnestly, perseveringly, believingly, until He accepts God's Word fully that it is a positive command and an immediate duty to be perfect.

*　　*　　*

31　The consciousness will soon grow strong of the utter impossibility of attempting obedience in human strength. The faith will grow that the word of command was simply meant to draw the soul to Him who gives what He asks.

The will of God is the expression of the Divine perfection.

1 Peter wanted to walk like Christ that he might get near
Christ. He did not say, "Lord, let me walk around the
sea here," but "Let me come to Thee." When Peter was in
the boat, what had he between him and the sea? A couple
of planks. But when he stepped out upon the water, what
had he between him and the sea? Not a plank, but the word
of the Almighty Jesus.

* * *

2 The Christian life compared to Peter walking on the
waves: nothing so difficult and impossible without Christ.
Nothing so blessed and safe with Christ. Peter walked back
to the boat without sinking again. Christ took him by the
hand and helped him; they were very near to each other, and
it was the nearness to His Lord that strengthened him. It is
possible to be far nearer Christ after failure than before.

* * *

3 How often we trouble about things, and about praying
for them, instead of going back to the root of things and
saying, "Lord, I only crave to be the receptacle of what the
will of God means for me; of the power and the gift and the
love and the Spirit of God."

You never can have too strong a will, but the trouble is
we do not give that strong will up to God, to make it a vessel
in which God can and will pour His Spirit, so as to fit it to
do splendid service for Himself. Does not God give us all
good gifts to enjoy? But the reality of the enjoyment is in
the giving back.

* * *

4 Have I not seen a mother give a piece of cake, and the
child offers her a piece? How she values the gift! Your
God, His Father's heart of love, longs to have you give Him
everything. He knows that every gift you bring will bind you
closer to Himself, every surrender will open your heart wider
to get more of His spiritual gifts.

When God's Word comes close to you and touches your

70

heart, remember that it is Christ, out of whose mouth goes the two-edged sword. It is Christ in His love coming to cut away the sin, that He may fill your heart with the blessing of God's love.

* * *

5 Do not ask, "Can I be kept from sinning if I keep close to Him?" but ask, "Can I be kept from sinning if He always keeps close to me?" and you see at once how safe it is to trust Him.

I may point men to Jesus as earnestly as I will, but it will avail little unless I lead them to believe that they must have the Holy Spirit in them to reveal Christ to them.

* * *

6 As our whole life becomes filled with the humbling, solemn, subduing presence of God, through the Holy Spirit, we shall walk about among people as men of God; not as men who vaguely preach about the Book, and what is in the Book, but who preach what they are, and what they have seen of Jesus.

EAGLE WINGS

7 When the Holy Spirit comes within us as the fire of God's love for souls, there will come to us an intensity and desire too deep for words. Then is the time when the Holy Spirit prays in us with groanings which cannot be uttered.

Love in the Spirit to each other, and, to all saints, prayer in the name of Jesus; God to be waited on and trusted, — this is a threefold cord which cannot be broken.

It is not always more work that is needed — some might with advantage work less; the main thing is the quality of work that is done.

* * *

8 What was to bring conviction that Jesus was the Christ? Love. That is what Christ said. "I pray that they may be one, that the world may know that Thou hast sent Me."

Not preaching, but love. Preaching is needed — praise God for what it does! — but love will do more.

* * *

9 The Son of God came to earth to prove that the love of God in heaven could stand the trial of life — every enmity, every shame, every suffering, and live through it all. It is your high privilege to have your heart filled with the heavenly love of Christ Jesus, and to carry it to this life.

* * *

10 I feel more and more deeply that you may have an earnest Christian, and yet his or her life be far below what God could make it, if he or she would wait for the Holy Spirit to get possession.

In our prayers continually, and in our life, let this thought be our joy and our strength: However ignorant I feel, and however feeble my words have been, the Spirit prays in me, and God, who searches the hearts, knows the mind of the Spirit.

* * *

11 How does God teach His eaglet children to use their wings? He comes and stirs up their nest with some tribulation or temptation. Why? Just as the eaglets, ready to sink, find the mother coming under them and carrying them, so the everlasting arms are stretched out underneath the soul that feels itself ready to perish. As the eaglet trusts the mother to carry it, so my God asks me to trust Him that He will bear me.

* * *

12 The everlasting God fainteth not, neither is weary. He giveth power to the faint, and to them that have no might He increaseth strength. If the everlasting God is never weary, you need never be weary, because your God is your strength. You have no strength but what God gives, and you can have all the strength that God can give.

Study and love your Bible, but remember it is God who

must give the orders, and you will fail if you take them from a book. Love your Bible, and fill your heart with it, but let God apply it in your daily life.

* * *

13 The great secret of a right waiting upon God is to be brought down to utter impotence. "I can do nothing of myself." Jesus said that, and He just waited upon God. Would not you like to occupy the very place that Jesus did before the Father and in the Father's heart? Would not you be willing to take that place, and to love every day as a man that has no might, but is utterly helpless, and just to wait upon God?

WAITING ON GOD

14 We must not only think of our waiting upon God, but also of what is more wonderful still — of God's waiting upon us. If He waits for us, then we are more than welcome.

Who can measure the difference between the great sun and that little blade of grass? Yet the grass has all of the sun it can need or hold. In waiting on God, His greatness and your littleness suit and meet each other most wonderfully.

* * *

15 Christ not only said "Abide in Me," but also "I in you."

The Epistles not only speak of us in Christ, but of Christ in us — the highest mystery of redeeming love. As we maintain our place in Christ day by day, God waits to reveal Christ in us.

* * *

16 There is such a danger of our being so occupied with the things that are coming more than with Him who is to come. Nothing but humble waiting on God can save us from mistaking intellectual study for the true love of Him and His appearing. Not when we are most occupied with prophetic subjects, but when in humility and love we are clinging close to our Lord and His brethren, are we in the Lord's place.

17 Instead of the tone of condemnation or of despair, wait
upon God in behalf of His erring children. If these fail
in doing it, give yourself doubly to it.

At times we are impatient with men and circumstances
that hinder us, or with ourselves and our slow progress in
the Christian life. If we truly wait upon God, we shall find
that it is with Him we are impatient, because He does not,
as soon as we could wish, do our bidding.

* * *

18 The activity of the mind in studying the Word or giving
expression to its thoughts in prayer may so engage us
that we do not come to the still waiting on the All Glorious
One.

MISCELLANEOUS EXTRACTS

19 If we seek above everything to be freed from our sin,
and to have the baptism of the Spirit, that Christ and
His will may have the complete mastery in us, if we seek it
for the sake of God's holiness, that He may be glorified, and
Christ be all, our happiness and our usefulness will come of
themselves.

* * *

20 In Scripture we have the words of daily life, in themselves without life or power. The mind can study and
utter them, but they bring neither help nor blessing. "The
letter killeth; the Spirit quickeneth." The fire of the Holy
Spirit takes them as its fuel, and makes them the power by
which the fire on the altars of our hearts is kept ever burning.

* * *

21 It is a terrible mistake to think that when once a man
is filled with the Spirit, persistent study of God's Word
and reverent whole-hearted submission to it is not as much
needed as before. "The priest shall burn wood on the altar
every morning."

22 Often Christian liberty is spoken of as freedom from restraint in sacrificing our will or the enjoyment of the world. Its real meaning is the very opposite. True love asks to be free from self and the world to bring its all to God. The truly free spirit asks, "How far am I free to follow Christ to the uttermost?"

* * *

23 Give up yourself to God's perfect love to work out His perfect will. For all He means you to do, He will surely give light and strength. The Throne of the Lamb is surely proof that there is no sure way for us to riches and honour than through His poverty.

* * *

24 The soul that in simplicity yields to the leading of her Lord will find that the fellowship of His suffering brings even here the fellowship of His glory. "Though He was rich, yet for your sakes He became poor, that ye through His poverty might be rich."

WITHIN

25 This is the chief mark and glory of the Son of God: that He lived and died, not for Himself, but for others. It was to do God's will that Christ came from heaven. It is to do God's will in you that He has entered your heart. Jesus won back for us the life man had been created for, with God dwelling in him, by giving to us His life, the very life He had lived.

* * *

26 All the sin of heathendom, all the sin of Christendom, is but the outgrowth of the one root — God dethroned, self enthroned, in the heart of man.

The mark of a kingdom is the presence of the king. With the Holy Spirit, Christ came down to be with His disciples as really and more nearly than when in the flesh. The disciples had their Lord with them as consciously as the angels in heaven. His presence made heaven all around and in them.

* * *

27 Think of the work Christ's disciples, simple fishermen, dared to undertake and were able to accomplish, — their weapon the despised gospel of the crucified Nazarene. See how the coming of the Kingdom brought a new power from heaven by which feeble men were made mighty through God, and the slaves of Satan were made God's holy children.

* * *

28 In the feebleness of the grave Jesus gained His throne. We need to die with Him, — that is the way to get delivered from self, the way to receive the heavenly life as a little child, and so to enter the Kingdom. The feebleness of Bethlehem and the manger, of Calvary and the grave, were Christ's way into the Kingdom; for us there is no other way.

* * *

29 As we seek to humble ourselves and to renounce all wish and all hope of being or doing good of ourselves, as we yield all our human ability and energy to the death in the confession that it is nothing but sinful and worthy of death, God's Spirit will make the power of Christ's death to sin work in us, we shall die with Him, and with Him be raised in newness of life. The new life will be the little child that receives the Kingdom.

* * *

30 How little we think that our heart was actually created that God might live there, that He might show forth His life and love there, and that our love and joy might be in Him alone. How little we know that just as naturally as we have the love of parents or of children filling our hearts and making us happy, we can have the living God, for whom the heart was made, dwelling there and filling it with His own blessedness and goodness.

31   "Father, here am I, for Thee to give as much in me a Christ's likeness as I can receive." Wait to hear Him say, "My child, I give thee as much of Christ as thy heart is open to receive."

The manna of one day was corrupt when the next day came. I must have every day fresh grace from heaven; and I obtain it only in direct waiting upon God Himself.

1 What is the difference between a dead Christ whom the women went to anoint and a living Christ? A dead Christ I must do everything for, a living Christ does everything for me.

In proportion as a man has, not as a sentiment or an aspiration, but in reality, the very Spirit and Presence of Jesus upon him, there comes out from him an unseen, silent influence. That secret influence is the holy presence of Jesus.

* * *

2 It is not your faith that will keep you standing, but it is a living Jesus, met every day in fellowship and worship and love. "Jesus, Thou hast told me to believe, to obey, to abide near Thee; is there anything more I need to secure the enjoyment of Thine abiding presence?" "I have redeemed thee a witness to go out into the world confessing Me before men." Work for Him who is worthy; His blessing and His presence will be found in the work.

* * *

3 You often try hard to trust God, and you fail. Why? Because you have not taken time first to see God. How can you trust God fully until you have met Him and known Him?

When God wanted to send any man upon His service, He first met him and talked with him and cheered him time after time. God appeared to Abraham seven or eight times, and gave to him one command after another, and so Abraham learned to obey Him perfectly. God appeared to Joshua and to Gideon, and they obeyed. Why are we not obedient? Because we have so little of this near intercourse with Jesus.

* * *

4 We read, "The Spirit of the Lord clothed Gideon." There is in the New Testament an equally wonderful text: "Put on the Lord Jesus Christ," that is, Clothe yourself with Christ Jesus. That does not only mean by inspiration of righteous-

78

ness outside of me, but to clothe myself with the living love
of the living Christ. He whom I have put on is as a garment
covering my whole being.

*   *   *

5   There are many Christians who know that they must not
        only believe in a crucified Christ, but in a living Christ,
and they try to grasp it, but it does not bring them a blessing.
Why? Because they want to *feel* it, and not to *believe* it.
They want to *work* for it, and *with efforts* get hold of it, instead of just *quietly* sinking down and believing: "Christ, the
living Jesus, He will do *everything* for us."

Just as a living child lives day by day in the arms of its
mother, and grows up year by year under a mother's eye, it
is a possibility that you can live every day and hour of your
life in fellowship with the Holy Jesus.

*   *   *

6   The great thing in prayer is to feel that we are putting
        our supplications into the bosom of omnipotent Love.
Before and above everything, let us take time ere we pray,
to realise the glory and presence of God. (Miscellaneous.)

"God first," is a motto often misunderstood. God first may
mean "I" second. God is thus first in order, but one of a
series of powers. The meaning of the words is really God
all — everything.

Christ cannot help coming in where there is a living faith,
a full faith. Do let us believe, because "all things are possible
to him that believeth." That is God's word.

*   *   *

7   What is to make a difference between Christ's disciples
        and other people? It is this: to be in fellowship with
Jesus every hour of the day. Christ is able in heaven now
to do what He could not do when He was on earth — to keep
in the closest fellowship with every believer throughout the
whole world. Why was my Lord Jesus taken up to heaven,

away from the life on earth? Because the life of earth is
confined to localities, but the life in heaven is a life in which
there is no limit, no bound, no locality. Christ was taken
up to heaven that in the power of the omnipresent God He
might be able to fill every individual here, and be with every
individual believer.

*   *   *

8 When we have Jesus with us, and when we go every
footstep with the thought that it is Jesus sends us, and
is helping us, then there will be brightness in our testimony,
and it will help other believers to understand. "I see why I
have failed: I took the word, the blessing, as I thought the
life, — but I was without the living Jesus."

Just as really as Christ was with Peter in the boat, just as
Christ sat with John at the table, as really can I have Christ
with me — more really, for they had their Christ in the body;
He was a man, an individual separate from them, but I may
have the glorified Christ in the power of the throne of God,
the omnipotent, omnipresent Christ.

THE MASTER'S INDWELLING

9 Why did God give the angels or man a self? God gave
me the power of self-determination that I might bring
this self every day, and say, "O God, work in it; I offer it to
Thee."

God's Word teaches us that God does not expect a man
to live as he ought for one minute, unless the Holy Spirit is
in him to enable him to do it.

Did ever a father or mother think, "For to-day I want my
child to love me?" No, they expect the love every day. So
God wants His child every moment to have a heart filled
with love of the Spirit.

*   *   *

10 Suppose a painter had a piece of canvas on which he
desired to work out some beautiful design; it does not

belong to him, and anyone has a right to take it and to use it for any other purpose; do you think the painter would bestow much work on that? No. Yet people want Jesus Christ to bestow His trouble upon them in taking away this temper, or that other sin, though in their hearts they have not yielded themselves utterly to His command and His keeping. If you will come and give your whole life into His charge, Christ Jesus is mighty to save; waits to fill you with His Spirit.

* * *

11 Fellowship with the Cross of Christ will be an unceasing denial of self, every hour and every moment, by the grace of God.

If I know that God is my God, not through man's teaching, not with my mind or my imagination, but in the living evidence which God gives in my heart, then I know that the Divine presence of my God will be so wonderful, and my God Himself so beautiful, so near, that I can live all my days and years a conqueror through Him that loved me.

* * *

12 The pointer helps to show the place on the map; it might be of fine gold, but we want to see what the pointer points out. This Bible is nothing but a pointer, pointing to God; and — may I say it with reverence — Jesus Christ came to point us, to show us the way. He died that He might bring us unto God.

The tree of one hundred years old — when it was planted God did not give it a stock of life by which to carry on its existence. Every year God clothes the tree with its foliage and its fruit, and that is what God is for — to work in us by His mighty operation, without one moment's ceasing.

* * *

13 Has God arranged that the light of that sun that will one day be burned up can come to you unconsciously, and shine in you blessedly and mightily? and is God not will-

ing, or not able, to let His light and His presence so shine
through you that you can walk all the day with God nearer
to you than anything in nature?

What is religion? Just as much as you have of God working in you. If you want more religion, more strength, more
fruitfulness, you must have more of God.

* * *

14 Israel passed through two stages — brought out from
Egypt into Canaan. If you would know the difference
between the life you have been leading, and the life you now
want to lead, look at the wilderness and Canaan. In the
wilderness, wandering; in Canaan, perfect rest: in the wilderness, want; in Canaan, plenty: in the wilderness, no victory;
in Canaan, they went from victory to victory.

* * *

15 The Holy Spirit is much spoken of in connection with
power; not so much spoken of in connection with the
graces, yet these are always more important than the gifts
of power: the holiness, the meekness, and the lovingness —
these are the true marks of the Kingdom.

The word "Lamb" must mean to us not only a sacrifice,
the shedding of blood, but the meekness of God, incarnate
upon earth, represented in the meekness and gentleness of
a little lamb.

* * *

16 It is good to be saved from the sins of stealing, murder-
ing, and every other evil; but a man needs above all
to be saved from what is the root of all sin — his self-will and
his pride.

If the windows of your room were closed the sun would
be on the outside of the building, streaming against the shut-
ters, but it could not enter. Leave the windows without shut-
ters, and the light can come in and fill the room. Even so
Jesus and His light, Jesus and His humility, are around you
on every side, longing to enter into your heart.

17 Christians do not know how much they rob Christ of
in reading so much of the literature of the world. They
are often so occupied with their newspapers that the Bible
gets a very small place. Bring this noble power of a mind
that can think heavenly, eternal, and infinite things, and lay
it at the feet of Jesus.

The Church of Christ suffers more to-day from trusting
in intellect, in sagacity, in culture, and in mental refinement
than from almost anything else. The spirit of the world
comes in, and men seek by their wisdom and by their knowledge to help the gospel, and they rob it of its crucifixion
mark.

* * *

18 I see Divine things, but cannot reach them; the self-
like is like an invisible plate glass. We are willing, we
are striving, and yet we are holding back something; we are
afraid to give up everything to God.

Your heart is too holy to have it filled with business; let
the business be in the head and under the feet, but let Christ
have the whole heart, and He will keep the whole life.

The Holy Spirit could pray a hundredfold more in us if
we were only conscious of our ignorance, because we would
then feel our dependence upon Him.

* * *

19 The smith puts his rod of iron into the fire. If he leaves
it there but a short time, it does not become red hot.
If he takes time, and leaves the rod in the fire, the whole
iron will become red hot with the heat that is in the fire. So
if we are to get the fire of God's holiness and love and power,
we must take more time with God in fellowship.

Ah, the blessedness of saying, "God and I!" But I find
in the Bible a more precious word still – it is, "God and not
I"; not God first, and I second; God is all, and I am nothing.

SPIRITUAL LIFE

20   We often speak of the wonderful revelation of the
Father's heart in His welcome to the prodigal son, but
we have a revelation of the Father's love far more wonderful
in what He says to the elder son, "Son, thou art ever with
Me, and all that I have is thine." What was the cause of the
terrible difference between the heart of the father and the
experience of the son? Unbelief.

If we are to experience a deepening of spiritual life, we
want to discover clearly what is the spiritual life that God
would have us live, and to ask whether we are living that
life, or if not, what hinders our living it fully.

*   *   *

21   The majority of Christians seem to regard the whole
of the Spirit's work as confined to conviction and con-
version; they hardly know that He came to dwell in our
hearts, and there reveal God in us.

Unbelief is the mother of disobedience and all other sins
and shortcomings — my temper, my pride, my unlovingness,
my worldliness. Though these differ in nature and form, yet
they all come from the one root, namely, that we do not believe in the freedom and fulness of the Divine gift of the
Holy Spirit to dwell in us and strengthen us, and fill us with
the life and grace of God all the day long.

*   *   *

22   Walk like Christ, and you shall always abide near
Christ. The presence of Christ invites you to come
and have unbroken fellowship with Him.

To walk through all the circumstances and temptations of
life is exactly like [Peter's] walking on the water — you have
no solid ground under your feet, but you have the Word of
God to rest on.

I remember the time in my spiritual life that, when I failed,
my only thought was to reproach and condemn myself. I
found it did not do me good; I learn from Peter [walking on

the water] that my work is, the very moment I fail, to say "Jesus, Master, help me," and the very moment I say that, Jesus does help me.

* * *

23 A father never sends his child away with the thought that he does not care about his child knowing that he loves him. He longs to have his child believe that he has the light of his father's countenance upon him all the day. If it be so with an earthly father, what think you of God? Does He not want every child of His to know that he is constantly living in the light of His countenance?

Who knows but what, just as Jesus said to the woman of Samaria, *"Give Me,"* because He wanted to say, *"I will give thee,"* He is *asking* you this gift to-day to lead you to see what is lacking in your spiritual life *(The Cross of Christ).*

* * *

24 The terrible history of mankind can never be rightly understood till we allow Scripture to teach us that, even as there is a purpose in God which overrules all, so there is, on the other hand, amid what appears nothing but a natural growth and development, an organised system and kingdom that holds rule over men, that keeps them in darkness, and uses them in its war against the kingdom of God's Son *(The Cross of Christ).*

* * *

25 When Christ came to save men, ere He entered His public ministry, He had first to meet God, and deal with Him. In His baptism He entered into fellowship with sinners, and gave Himself to fulfil all righteousness; in the vision of the opened heaven and the descending dove, as in the voice of the Father, He received the seal of the Divine approval. He then had to meet the tempter, through whom Adam had fallen; only then could He begin His ministry among men. As definitely as Christ in the work of salvation had to deal with God and with man, had He to deal with Satan too.

85

There was no salvation possible, but as Satan's power was acknowledged, and met, and overthrown *(The Cross of Christ)*.

* * *

26 Is it possible that the lack of Christ's poverty is the cause of our lack of His riches? Is there not a needs-be that we not only think of the one side, "For your sakes He became poor;" but as much of the other, "For His sake I suffer the loss of all things?" *(The Poverty of Christ)*.

* * *

27 The poverty of Christ has been to tens of thousands the assurance that He could feel for them: that even as with Him, earthly need was to be the occasion of heavenly help; the school for a life of faith; and the experience of God's faithfulness the path to heavenly riches *(The Poverty of Christ)*.

* * *

28 As it was with the fruit good for food and pleasant to the eye, sin entered the world, so the great power of the world over men is in the cares, and possessions, and enjoyments of this life. Christ came to win the world back to God. He did so by refusing every temptation to accept its gifts or seek its aid. Of this protest against the worldly spirit, its self-pleasing and its trust in the visible, the poverty of Christ was one of the chief elements *(The Poverty of Christ)*.

* * *

29 Christ overcame the world, first, in the temptations by which its prince sought to ensnare Him; then and through that, in its power over us *(The Poverty of Christ)*.

In Paul's wonderful life, as in his writings, he proves what weight it gives to the testimony concerning eternal things, when the witness can appeal to his own experience of the infinite satisfaction which the unseen riches can give *(The Poverty of Christ)*.

30 In monastic days, men expected from poverty what only the Spirit of Christ, revealing itself in poverty, could accomplish. Here was the failure *(The Poverty of Christ).*

Christ separated for Himself a band of men, who were to live with Him in closest fellowship, in entire conformity to His life, under His immediate training. These three conditions were indispensable for their receiving the Holy Spirit, for being true witnesses to Him and the life which He had lived, and would impart to men *(The Poverty of Christ).*

1 After a sermon or a conversation a soul had a little light,
but speedily again lost it. He did not still keep the promises anew before him, that unbelief might not again obtain
the upper hand.

The question must be continually repeated, "What does
God require me to believe?" and in the face of whatever
weakness, must the answer be at His feet: "Lord, I believe —
I will believe."

Martha did not yet believe everything, but what she believed that she spoke out before the Lord. She believed in
Him as the Son of the living God; this was the principal thing
and the source of greater faith. She was diligent in prayer,
that her faith would be strengthened and become capable of
receiving yet more and more.

*   *   *

2 He who knows that there is a Spirit to actuate to faith
knows also that man may, with spirit and hope, strive
to exercise faith.

The more fully the soul believes, the more clear becomes
the revelation of the Spirit; the more fully the Spirit works
in it, the more does the soul grow in the life of faith and
confidence. Thus we may have the Spirit of faith.

No sooner is faith cultivated in a one-sided fashion, without a growing conscientiousness of the casting off of little
sins, and the sanctification of the whole heart and walk, than
it becomes a work merely of the understanding or the feeling.

*   *   *

3 We teach our children to utter words which they do not
yet fully understand, in the confidence that the thoughts
and feelings expressed in them will be gradually imprinted
on their hearts. Idle and sinful words are at the outset
uttered carelessly, become rooted in the heart, and bear their
own fruits. And what do we not observe in prayer? That the
soul uttering "Thy will be done," although the heart does not
as yet fully assent, shall at last by the very use of the expression, submit to the casting out of the unwilling disposition.

4 Sincerity is that attitude of the soul, in virtue of which we present ourselves to the Lord just as we are, neither better nor worse.

The Word has not yet defined how deeply one must feel sin before one may come to Jesus; it has fixed no measure. The first sense of need must bring us to Him. Remaining apart from Jesus is just the way to make the sense of sin less.

* * *

5 Always the closer to the light, the more visible the impurity; the nearer to the Holy One, the stronger the sense of unworthiness; the more blessed with grace, the deeper the conviction of sin.

You wound Him in the most tender point when you doubt if His grace is indeed for you, and so drag its greatness and trustworthiness into doubt.

Just because you fear your own unfaithfulness, you must place your confidence in God's faithfulness.

* * *

6 It is not my business to be anxious, and to say how God's Word can be fulfilled. The Lord will see to it.

If the Lord has given no promises for you, then it cannot be your duty to believe. But as surely as the Word says "Believe," is there also a promise which you must believe.

There is no lost one so far lost that Jesus cannot find him and cannot save him.

* * *

7 Give yourself to the Lord Jesus just as you are. Not as an offering that is worthy of Him, not as one who is already His friend. No, surrender yourself to Him as one that is dead, whom He has to make alive, as an enemy whom He must forgive.

With one, it is trial in the physical life; with another, trial in the family; with another, vexation of soul; with still more, hidden conflict with sin. But trial there must be; for so long as the flesh has everything agreeable, the soul will never wholly and with power cleave to the Lord.

* * *

8 When the Lord is to lead a soul to great faith, He leaves its prayers unheard. So it was with the Canaanite woman. He answered her not one word, and when He did at length reply to her, the answer was still more unfavourable than His silence. This is always the way. If the answer came immediately His gifts would occupy its attention so much, that it would overlook the Lord Himself. It must first stand upon its Lord and what He has provided, without any answer; He and His Word are to suffice for it.

* * *

9 The more you simply take the Word, read and read again the message of God, contemplate one after another the promises with which God has made it sure that the Saviour is for every sinner, the sooner shall you feel constrained to say, "It is true; God says it; I must believe it."

Just as water ever seeks and fills the lowest place, so the moment God finds the creature abased and empty, His glory and power flow in to exalt and to bless. "He that humbleth himself" — that must be our one care — "shall be exalted," — that is God's care; by His mighty power, and in His great love He will do it.

* * *

10 Then believed they His words; they sang His praise. In believing, the soul wholly forgets itself, and, with undivided energy, looks to God and hears Him; in thanksgiving, the soul must be entirely occupied with the adoration of the Godhead, the contemplation of His goodness, the consideration of His ways. Accordingly the more the mind is exercised in this work, and is taken up with the thought of all this, the more shall there be fixed and rooted in it the conviction that the Lord is truly a God on whom it is its duty to rely. If thanksgiving, the express mention of His omnipotence, His love, His faithfulness, His perfection shall fill the soul, the result cannot but be that the soul shall suffer it to be concentrated on God. He that has but a single word of such a God to build upon, has enough.

* * *

11 If you are still unconverted, thank Him that you are still not in hell.

Praising and believing are one.

There must be a continual repetition of the act of faith, cleaving fast to the Word of God until He bestows the blessing.

You also shall be born again by the Living Word, and be cleansed from your sin. It does not lie in you, nor even in the Word regarded in itself, but in the faithfulness of God, who has said, "He that believeth shall not be ashamed."

Paul always speaks of the works of the law; James of the works of faith. The works of the law are done of the personal power of man, to fulfil the law of God in order to merit His favour. The works of faith are done for the confirmation and the perfecting of faith, out of the power which God gives and not to merit anything.

* * *

12 He who with faithful perseverance continues day by day in the use of the Word, even when he does not at once observe blessing from it, shall experience increase of faith, although unobserved and slow, yet certain and sure. Many are often content in the morning with the general reading of the Word in the household, apart from private meditation with prayer. The reading of a chapter once a day is, as a rule, not sufficient. No, let all that truly desire to increase in faith, see to it that they endeavour in the morning hour to gather for the day manna on which to ruminate. He that goes out in the morning without nutriment, comes home weary in the evening, with but little desire to eat. He who does not in the morning first lay up the Word in his heart, is not to be surprised if the world assumes the first and the chief place in his heart, for he has neglected the only means of being in advance of the world.

*   *   *

13 Readiness and ability for any work is not given before the work, but only through the work, thus only after we begin to work. The child that learns to run, begins before he can readily do it, and learns in the effort.

God gives commands for which we have previously no power, yet requires obedience with full right; because when we set ourselves towards obedience, strength will be given along with this incipient activity.

*   *   *

14 Whenever the devil is bent on keeping back anyone from salvation, he has merely to keep him back also from faith. Luke 8:12.

The heart cannot at the same time move towards God and away from God, cannot equally desire the Word and sin.

When one remembers how superficially the Word is read, what little pains is taken to understand the Word, to take into the heart and keep there every day that which should be fitted to strengthen faith, one feels how lightly and easily the Word is taken away; it costs the devil little trouble.

*   *   *

15 Even the devil knows this: where the Word dwells in the heart, there faith comes.

Before that Word the evil one retreats, as before the "It is written" out of Jesus' mouth: with and by that Word the Lord God and His Spirit come to the soul.

The Lord who gives the Word will also give the faith to receive it; He who has given the promise will also bestow the fulfilment. Set yourself to believe in the joyful confidence: it is given.

Let every experience of failure, of unbelieving, of insensibility, convince you how unfortunate it would be if you had to believe of yourself; how blessed that you may look to God for it.

HUMILITY

16 Humility is not something which we bring to God, or He bestows; it is simply the sense of entire nothingness, which comes when we see how truly God is all, and in which we make way for God to be all.

"Blessed are the poor in spirit, for theirs is the kingdom of heaven: blessed are the meek, for they shall inherit the earth." The poor who have nothing in themselves, to them the kingdom comes. The meek, who seek nothing in themselves, theirs the earth shall be. The blessings of heaven and earth are for the lowly.

* * *

17 No outward instructions, not even of Christ Himself; no argument, however convincing; no sense of the beauty of humility, however deep; no personal resolve or effort, however sincere and earnest, can cast out the devil of pride. Nothing can avail but this, that the new nature in its Divine humility be revealed in power to take the place of the old, to become as truly our very nature as that ever was.

* * *

18 The only humility that is really ours is not that which we try to show before God in prayer, but that which we carry with us, and carry out in our ordinary conduct. The insignificancies of daily life are the importances and the tests of eternity, because they prove what really is the spirit that possesses us. It is in our most unguarded moments that we really show and see what we are. To know the humble man, to know how he behaves, you must follow him in the common course of daily life.

19 The believer is often in danger of aiming at and rejoicing in the more manly virtues — boldness, joy, contempt of the world, zeal, self-sacrifice. Even the old Stoics practised these. While the deeper, diviner graces, those which Jesus first taught upon earth, because He brought them from heaven, those which are more distinctly connected with His cross and the death of self — poverty of spirit, meekness, humility, lowliness — are scarcely thought of or valued.

*   *   *

20 It is the soul in which God the Creator, as the All of the creature in its nothingness, — God the Redeemer in His grace, as the All of the sinner in his sinfulness, is waited for and trusted and worshipped, that will find itself so filled with His presence that there will be no place for self, "The haughtiness of man shall be brought low, and the Lord alone shall be exalted in that day."

*   *   *

21 Pride makes faith impossible. "How can ye believe who receive glory from one another?" Faith and humility are at root one. We can never have more of true faith than we have of true humility. We may indeed have strong intellectual conviction of the truth, but pride makes the living faith which has power with God an impossibility.

There are two cases in which Jesus spoke of a great faith. Had not the centurion, at whose faith He marvelled, saying, "I have not found so great faith, no, not in Israel," spoken, "I am not worthy that Thou shouldst come under my roof"? Had not the mother to whom he spoke, "Woman, great is thy faith," accepted the name of dog and said, "Yea, Lord, yet the dogs eat of the crumbs"?

*   *   *

22 All God's dealings with man are characterised by two stages: preparation—when command and promise train men for a higher stage; fulfilment — when faith inherits the promise, and enjoys what it had so often struggled for in vain.

94

God, who had been the Beginning, ere man rightly knew Him or fully understood what His purpose was, is longed for and welcomed as the End, the All in all.

* * *

23 Humility becomes us as creatures, as sinners, as saints. The first we see in the heavenly hosts, unfallen man, Jesus as Son of Man. The second appeals to us in our fallen state, and points out the only way through which we can return to our right place as creatures. In the third we have the mystery of grace, which teaches us that as we lose ourselves in the overwhelming greatness of redeeming love, humility becomes to us the consummation of everlasting blessedness and adoration.

* * *

24 What is Jesus' incarnation but His heavenly humility, His emptying Himself and becoming man? What is His life on earth but humility, His taking the form of a servant? What is His atonement but humility? He humbled Himself and became obedient unto death. What is His ascension but humility exalted to the throne and crowned with glory? "He humbled Himself, therefore God highly exalted Him."

Only humility leads to perfect death; only death perfects humility. Humility and death are in their very nature one: humility is the end; in death the fruit is ripened to perfection.

The Christian's life ever bears the twofold mark; its roots striking in true humility deep into the grave of Jesus, the death to sin and self: its head lifted up in resurrected power to the heaven where Jesus is.

* * *

25 We know the law of human nature: acts produce habits, habits produce dispositions, dispositions form the will, and the rightly formed will is character. It is not otherwise in the work of grace.

It is only in the possession of God that I lose myself. As it is in the height and breadth and glory of the sunshine that

95

the littleness of the mote playing in its beams is seen, even so humility is the taking our place in God's presence to be nothing but a mote dwelling in the sunshine of His love.

* * *

26 Let us ask whether we regard a reproof just or unjust, a reproach from friend or enemy, an injury or trouble, or difficulty into which others bring us, as above all an opportunity of proving how Jesus is all to us, how our own pleasure or honour are nothing. It is indeed blessed, the deep happiness of heaven, to be so free from self that whatever is said of us, or done to us, is lost and swallowed up in the thought that Jesus is all.

* * *

27 With the abiding in Christ everything is yielded to the power of His life in us, that it may exercise its sanctifying influence even on ordinary wishes and desires. His Holy Spirit breathes through our whole being; and our desires, as the breathings of the Divine life, are in conformity with the Divine will, and are fulfilled. Abiding in Christ renews and sanctifies the will. We ask what we will, and it is given us *(Abide in Christ).*

* * *

28 The peace of Christ is not something that He puts into your heart, and that you must keep that it may keep you. If the peace of God is to rule in my heart, it is because the God of peace Himself is there. Can you separate the light of the sun from the sun? You cannot have the peace of Christ apart from Christ *(Northfield Echoes).*

* * *

29 In Revelation we read of only two churches in which there was nothing to blame. In each of the others you find the word "repent." There could be no overcoming, and receiving a blessing, unless they repented. Let us repent on behalf of the Church of Christ, and God will make us feel

how much our own sins are part of the trouble. Then God
will give His Holy Spirit, and will encourage us to feel that
He will revive His work *(Northfield Echoes)*.

*   *   *

30 Every man acts always according to the idea he has
of his state. A king acts like a king if he is conscious
of his kingship. So I cannot live the life of a true believer
unless I am conscious every day that I am dead in Christ.
He died unto sin. I am united with Him, and I am dead
to sin *(Northfield Echoes)*.

*   *   *

31 Joseph was sold by his brethren, but he saw God in it,
and was content. Christ was betrayed by Judas, con-
demned by Caiaphas, and given over to execution by Pilate,
but in it all Christ saw God and was content. All that Poti-
phar had, he left in Joseph's hands. He could now do the
king's business with two hands and an undivided heart. Will
you leave all in Jesus' hands, and so be free to attend to the
King's business? Every temptation will bring you a blessing
if Jesus has charge of everything *(Northfield Echoes)*.

1 As each seed bears fruit after its kind, and of its very own nature, and the fruit in its turn again becomes a seed, so the Spirit of Christ was the hidden seed-life of which the Cross was the fruit. And the Cross again became the seed of which the Spirit is the fruit. And once again, the Spirit in the believer, and the Church as a whole, is the seed of which the conformity to the Cross and the death of Christ is the fruit. It is the great work of the Spirit to fill the world with this blessed seed, everywhere to reproduce the image and the likeness of the crucified Lord. The highest work of the Spirit is to reveal the Cross — the wisdom and the power of God.

* * *

2 It is as the Church proves itself the very body of the Lord Jesus, by showing forth the very same life there was in Him, that His power as Head can freely flow through her. It is as her determination not to know anything but Jesus Christ and Him crucified is seen in her being crucified with Christ, being crucified to the world, that His resurrection, joy and power can be manifested in her. In the Church the world must hear and see Jesus Christ and Him crucified.

Such intense devotion to the Cross and the crucified Lord as works inward and outward conformity to Him, is the first requisite of the gospel minister, if Paul is at all to be counted a model for imitation. It was the one secret of his ministry and his power.

* * *

3 The confidence with which the preacher speaks rests not on a message or a book alone — that never alone can enable him to speak as one who knows and witnesses. His commission is a living one, — in such measure as the Holy Spirit has revealed the Cross to him and in him, can he testify in power of what it is and does. The mystery of God is Christ in us, the hope of glory; not a thought, but a life with its knowledge, not that of the mind, but of the renewed spirit. The preacher can speak the mystery with authority when he knows that the office of God the Holy Spirit is to give the mystery entrance into the heart, however dark. The word of Divine authority and power brings men into God's presence, wakens a sense of want and desire, and inspires faith in an unseen but present deliverance.

* * *

4 The Cross is the greatest of all mysteries – their sum and centre. In it we see the mystery of God – the Father ordaining, the Son bearing, the Spirit revealing and honouring it. The mystery of man – his sin, rejecting Christ; his curse, Christ forsaken of God; his worth, God's Son dying for him. The mystery of love – God offering Himself to bear the sin and the suffering of man, and making man one with Himself. The mystery of death and of life – death reigning, death conquered, and made the gateway of life eternal. The mystery of redemption – the Cross with its sin and shame made the power that conquers the sinner, and, while it humbles and slays, that wakens his hope and highest enthusiasm. The mystery of God's wisdom casting down reason and filling the heart with the light of God and eternity.

* * *

5 Just as I cannot by any possibility know the taste or nourishing power of a food except by partaking of it, so there is no way of knowing Christ Jesus and Him crucified but by receiving Him into my life, and being made partaker of the disposition that animated His life and His Cross. Jesus Christ is the revelation of the life of God as it appears and acts in human nature. In the Holy Spirit, Jesus Christ is come from heaven to live and act in His disciples. We only know Jesus Christ as far as we partake of His nature and life and Spirit.

Is it any wonder that the preaching of the gospel is not more effectual when men forget that they are preaching a Divine mystery to those whom the god of this world hath blinded? The darkness of heart is a supernatural one, — the power that can enlighten is not the force of reason or argument, not the persuasion of culture or appeal, but the supernatural enlightening and quickening of the Holy Spirit. "It is God who hath shined in our hearts, to give the knowledge of the glory of God, in the face of Jesus Christ." The light of God shining in the heart alone can witness to the mystery of His love in the Cross. The great hindrance to the preaching of the Cross is a worldly spirit. The worldly spirit proves itself in nothing so much as in that which is its chief boast — its wisdom.

*   *   *

6 Have we not often sought by earnest thought to enter more deeply into the significance of the Cross? Have we not, as we got a glimpse of some aspect of its glory, gone from book to book to find out what it really means? Have not some given up hope that words like "I am crucified with Christ," "the world is crucified to me," "baptized into His death," "dead unto sin, and alive unto God in Christ," should ever become truly intelligible and helpful? Is not the reason of all this that we want to grasp the hidden wisdom of God with our little mind, and forget that the Holy Spirit wants to give it into the heart, and into the inner life, in a way and in a power that passeth knowledge?

The Cross brings to each one who believes in it the death that is "the gate of life." There is given through it the fulness and the power of the Spirit.

*   *   *

7 Remember that His Holy Spirit, His crucifixion Spirit, is in you, not first of all to give you clear or beautiful thoughts, which might delude you, but to communicate the very temper and disposition out of which the Cross grew.

When the Church has to complain of the withholding of the saving power, the reason must be that the crucifixion spirit in which the saving power finds its life, is wanting. It must be because the Church is not saying as Paul said, "I

came not with excellency of speech, or of wisdom, proclaiming the wisdom of God, for I determined not to know anything save Christ and Him crucified."

In that life of our Lord the most remarkable thing, its great
feature, its Divine mystery and glory, was His being crucified
on the Cross. He proved how life has no object but as it can
be made to serve God's will; how suffering and sacrificing all
is the highest and most well-pleasing religion and obedience;
how there is no way out of the life into which He has brought
us into the glory of God, but through dying to it.

The Cross means the sacrifice of all. To know the Crucified in the conformity of His death, we need to count all
things loss. The Cross demands the life. It is a ministry that
comes not in excellency of speech or wisdom, but boasts in
the "weakness" and the "foolishness" of the Cross that will
convict the world of its sin and its earthliness, and will lift
men up to a supernatural life.

*   *   *

8 We must ever return to our Lord, and men like His
servant Paul, and see what the elements are that go to
make up the crucifixion spirit. A deep sense of the sinfulness of sin, and of the righteousness of God's judgment on it;
an entire separation from the world, and a clear protest
against its apostasy from God, under the power of the god
of this world; a life-long surrender of our own will and
pleasure, as a sacrifice to God to work out His will in us;
a parting with all excellency of speech and wisdom, as making the Cross of none effect; a passion of love for the souls
of men, giving its life as completely up for them as Christ
did; the acceptance of death to all that is of human nature
as sinful and under the curse that the life and power of
heaven may work all in us; — this was the spirit that animated Paul, as it animated Jesus Christ.

*   *   *

9 Accept your sense of ignorance heartily; depend entirely
upon the Spirit to reveal the hidden mystery in "the hid-

den part"; count confidently on the work He is doing in you; keep your heart set on your crucified Lord in meditation and worship, with an increasing sense of how little you know or understand, — and the Blessed Spirit will do His hidden work where you can see it. Trust Him fully: He will do it.

The Cross is the wisdom of God in a mystery: the Spirit of God alone can reveal it. How this would teach us how to preach the Cross aright. A mystery must be accepted on authority. The apostle or preacher holds a Divine commission to tell men in the name of God what they do not know, what they cannot understand, until they first bow before God to accept it.

* * *

10 The spirit of the world, apparently honouring and proclaiming the Cross, is the great cause why the Church's preaching is so little in demonstration and in power. It robs the Cross of what is its chief glory, that it is the wisdom of God in a mystery, with the Holy Spirit from heaven as its only interpreter.

The sense of mystery is of the very essence of true worship. Though at first it burdens and bows down, it soon becomes as the high mountain air, in which faith breathes free and strong. The sense of mystery brings the soul under the power of the Invisible and Eternal, the Holy and Divine.

The Cross — the wisdom of God in a mystery; let us bow and worship and wait in deep humility. What God devised, God will reveal. We are come to Mount Zion; the Lamb is the light thereof. As we adore what we cannot, would not understand, the Spirit will impart what God hath bestowed. And we shall learn to walk as men who know that what ear hath not heard, and what heart cannot conceive, God is working out in them that love Him.

* * *

11 Let anyone who desires to be brought into fellowship with his crucified Lord, hold fast the words, "The wisdom of God in a mystery: God hath revealed it to us by His

Spirit." As you gaze upon the Cross, and long for conformity
to Him, be not weary or fearful because you cannot express
in words what you seek. Ask Him to plant the Cross in
your heart. Believe in Him, the Crucified and now Living
One, to dwell within you, and breathe His own mind there.
It is not alone the work of Christ, but the living Christ Himself, as the Crucified One that the gospel reveals. A sinner
often wearies himself in vain in trying to take hold of the
work of Christ and its blessings. When he sees that it is
Jesus Christ Himself, and Him crucified, he has to trust, he
finds One who takes charge and works all in him.

LET US DRAW NIGH

12 How much your life depends on your relation to the
promises. Connect the promises with the Promiser, the
Promiser with His unchanging faithfulness as God, and your
hope will become a glorying in God through Jesus Christ
our Lord.

Confession strengthens hope; what we utter becomes more
real to us. It glorifies God. It helps and encourages those
around us. Fulness of faith and fulness of hope make the
true heart. Because we have nothing in ourselves, and God
is to be all, and to do all, our whole attitude is to be to look
up to Him, expecting and receiving what He is to do. The
entrance into the Holiest is given us as priests, there to be
filled with the Spirit and the love of Christ, and to go out
and bring Christ's blood to others.

No effort of thy will can bring forth love. It must be given
thee from above.

*   *   *

13 The knowledge of what Christ has won for me, the
entrance into the Heavenlies; of the work He did to
win it, the shedding of His blood, — all this is very precious.
But there is something better still; the living, loving Son of

God is there personally, to make me partaker of all the blessedness that God has for me.

In the court there were the brazen altar and the laver. At the one the priest sprinkled the blood, at the other he washed ere he entered the Holy Place. At the installation of the Passover they were first washed and then sprinkled with blood. In the great Day of Atonement the high priest had to wash ere he entered the Holiest. The Word and water are joined together (Eph. 5:26; John 13:10; 15:3), because the Word is the external manifestation of what must rule our whole outer life. The liberty of access, the cleansing the Blood gives, can only be enjoyed in a life of which every action is cleansed by the Word.

* * *

14 Nothing will help us to keep ourselves unspotted in this world but the Spirit that was in Christ, that looked upon His body as prepared by God for His service. It is for every man as for the Master to put away sin by the sacrifice of self. Not burnt sacrifices, but the sacrifice of our own will to do God's will, is what delights God.

Our eating and drinking, our sleeping, our clothing, our labour and relaxation, influence our spiritual life. They often interrupt the fellowship we seek to maintain. Through the body Satan conquered in Paradise; in the body he tempted Christ. It was in sufferings of the body that Christ was perfected.

* * *

15 Where God is, is heaven, the heaven of His presence includes this earth too. Into the Holiest, into the light of God's holy presence and love, into full union with Him, the soul can enter by faith that makes us one with Christ, and abide continually because Jesus abideth continually.

The boldness to enter into the Holiest is not a conscious feeling of confidence; it is the objective God-given right of entrance of which the Blood assured us. The measure of our boldness is the worth God attaches to the Blood of Jesus.

Which is now greater in your sight: your sin, or the Blood of Jesus? There can be but one answer. As your sin has hitherto kept you back, let the Blood now bring you nigh and give you the power to abide. The Blood has put away the thought of sin from God. He remembers it no more for ever. The Blood has put away the thought of sin in me too, the evil conscience that condemns me. The better things which the Blood speaks in heaven, it speaks in my heart too.

*   *   *

16 The truth of Jesus' heavenly Priesthood is so often powerless because we look upon it as an external, distant thing, a work going on in heaven above us. The one cure is to know that our Great Priest over the house of God — and we are His house too — is the glorified Jesus, who makes His presence and power in heaven by the Holy Spirit to be as real within us here, as it is above us there.

There are seasons for Bible reading, prayer, churchgoing. But how speedily and naturally the heart turns to worldly things. It is not the worship of a true heart. God asks the affection, the will; the head and the heart are in partnership, but the heart must lead. Our religion has been too much of the head — hearing, reading, thinking. Draw nigh, it never says with a clear head, but with a true heart.

The action of the Blood in heaven is increasing. Even so will it be in the soul that enters in to live amid the cares, engagements, companionships of daily life in an inner sanctuary, where everything acts in the power of the upper world.

*   *   *

17 There are outer court Christians, Israelites who trust in Christ who died on Calvary. Beyond these are Christian priests who know the power of the Blood for service. Then come those high priests who know that the Holy Spirit applies the Blood in such power, that it indeed brings to the life in the inner sanctuary, in the full and abiding joy of God's presence.

The surrender of all becomes only possible when the soul sees how truly Jesus engages to put His own delight in God's law into the heart, to give the will and the strength to live in all God's will.

Faith accepts the promise in its divine reality; Hope goes forward to examine and rejoice in the treasures which Faith has accepted. Faith will perhaps be most tried when God wants most to bless. Hope is the daughter of Faith, the messenger it sends out to see what is to come. It is Hope that becomes the strength and support of Faith.

THE LORD'S SUPPER

18   One chief cause why some do not grow more in grace is that they do not take time to hold converse with the Lord in secret. Christians, give yourselves, give your Lord time to transfer His heavenly thoughts to your inner, spiritual life. Take time to remain before Him until He has made His Word living and powerful in your souls. Then does it become the life and power of your life.

Books can become a blessing to the reader only when they bring him always to that portion of God's Word which is treated of, in order that he may meditate further upon it himself, and receive it for himself, as from the mouth of God.

* * *

19   To find food for angels: for this only one word was necessary. But to prepare for man a banquet upon this accursed earth, a banquet of heavenly food: that cost God much, — nothing less than the life and blood of His Son, to take away the curse and open up to them the right and the access to heavenly blessings.

The greater the work is that a man undertakes, the more important is the preparation. Four days before the Passover the Israelite had to make his preparations. The Lord Jesus also desired that care should be taken to obtain an upper room, furnished and ready, where the Passover might be prepared. When I am called upon to meet my God and to sit down at His table, I will see to it that I do not approach it unprepared.

* * *

20 Great thoughts of Jesus, and large expectations of what His love will do, will set the heart aglow and be the best preparation for meeting Himself. To have a deep-rooted renunciation of myself, in order to be willing to live through Jesus alone, — this is the attitude of a soul which leads to a blessed observance of the Supper.

Even as the little weak infant that does not know how to eat is fed by its mother's hand, so will Jesus break for me the bread of heaven, and impart to me what I have need of.

* * *

21 There is nothing on earth that awakens love and rouses it to activity so powerfully as the thought of being desired and loved. Jesus' desire is toward me. Believe and ponder this wonderful thought, until you feel drawn with overmastering force to give yourself over to Jesus for the satisfaction of His desire toward you: then shall you, too, be satisfied.

* * *

22 The more the believer really despairs of himself, the more glorious will Christ become in his eyes. The more keenly he feels every sin, the more will Jesus become to him. Every sin is a need that calls for Jesus. By the confession of sin you point out to Him the spot where you are wounded, and where He must exhibit the healing power of His blood. Every sin that you confess is an acknowledgment of something which Jesus must cast out, and the place of which He is bound to fill up with one of the lovely gifts of His holiness. Every sin that you confess is a new reason why you should believe more and ask more, and a new reason why Jesus should bless you.

The very same light that enables you to feel the curse of sin more deeply, enables you also to discern the perfect and final victory over it. The experience *utterly lost,* prepares the way for the experience *utterly redeemed.*

* * *

23 The *sin offering,* by which atonement was made, was the type of the sacrifice of Christ alone. "He was made sin for us." The *burnt offering,* which had to be wholly consumed by fire on the altar, as a symbol of entire devotedness to the service of God, was the type alike of the sacrifice of Christ and of the sacrifice of believers in which they surrender themselves to the Lord. The idea of thank offering is exhibited more fully to the apprehension in the feast of *thank offering,* and in the fellowship that ensued.

* * *

24 Of the *sin offering,* by which atonement was made, the priests might eat as a token of their fellowship with God through the atonement. The Lord's Supper is our fellowship in the perfect sacrifice of Jesus Christ, which has done away with sin for ever. Of the *thank offering,* in which dedication to God was shown forth, the offerer himself might also eat, in recognition of his fellowship with God in this dedication. The Lord's Supper is a communion with Christ, not only because He offered Himself up for us, but because in and with Him we offer ourselves to the Father, with all that we have.

My Saviour, do Thou Thyself come into me; my faith can only be the fruit of what Thou givest me to know of Thyself.

* * *

25 He loves us so dearly that He sets great store by our love. Our love is to Him His happiness and joy. He requires it from us with a holy strictness. So truly has the eternal Love chosen us, that it longs to live in our remembrance every day. Thou knowest, Lord, it is not by any force my heart can be taught to remember Thee.

If by Thy love Thou dwellest in me, thinking of Thee becomes a joy, — no effort or trouble, but the sweetest rest.

When I hear the glad tidings that Christ died for sin, I obtain courage to say, Sin is mine; and Christ, who died for sin, died also for me. When I first look on sin, I can make bold to say that Christ is mine. The forgiveness of sin is, as it were, the pledge of entrance into the whole riches of the grace of God.

* * *

26 All knowledge of the truth, and all acquaintance with the gospel, are of no avail without the personal appropriation of that short phrase, *"For me."* And that word of man has, on the other hand, its foundation in the word of Jesus, *"For you."*

As by the circulation of the blood every member of our body is kept unceasingly in the most vital connection with the others, so the body of Christ can increase and become strong only when, in the loving interchange of the fellowship of the Spirit and of love, the life of the Head can flow unhindered from member to member.

* * *

27 To be thankful for what I have received, and for what my Lord has prepared, is the surest way to receive more. A joyful, thankful Christian shows that God can make those who serve Him truly happy. He stirs up others to praise God along with him. If my Saviour went singing from the Lord's Table to the conflict in Gethsemane, may I, in the joy of His redemption, follow Him with thanksgiving into every conflict to which He calls me. The nearer to the throne of God, the more thanksgiving. In heaven they praise God day and night; a Lord's Supper pervaded by the spirit of thanksgiving is a foretaste of it.

28 Life must be fed with life. In corn, the life of nature is hid, and we enjoy the power of that life in bread. It was to make heavenly life accessible to us that the Son of God died like the seed corn in the earth, that His body was broken like the bread grain. It is to communicate this life to us and to make it our own that He gives Himself to us in the Supper.

* * *

29 "I have meat to eat that ye know not of." Jesus had a hidden manna that He received from the Father, and that was the secret of His wonderful power. The nutriment of His life He received from God in heaven. The doing of God's will was for Jesus the bread of heaven; and since I have now received Jesus Himself as my heavenly bread, He teaches me to eat what He Himself ate; He teaches me to do the will of God.

It was when Abraham returned from the campaign for the deliverance of Lot, that Melchisedec, the priest of the Most High God, set before him bread and wine. "To him that overcometh," says Jesus — to him that works, and strives, and overcomes — "will I give to eat of the hidden manna."

Heavenly food brings heavenly strength, and heavenly strength brings heavenly work.

* * *

30 It is one of the characteristics of God's work, that with Him the end is as certain as the beginning. He has sought me and made me His own, and what He has thus done to me points back to that which He did for me. He gave His own Son, and by His blood He bought for Himself as His own possession. And that again points back to eternity. He chose me and loved me before the foundation of the world. My soul, ponder what this means: "He has begun." Then shalt thou be able joyfully to exclaim, "The Lord will perfect that which concerneth me."

1 It is where parents love the Lord their God with all
their heart and strength that the human love will be
strengthened and sanctified. It is only parents who are willing to live really consecrated lives, entirely given up to God,
to whom the promise and the blessing can come fully true.

An angel of the Lord had appeared to Manoah's wife to
predict the birth of Samson; this angel's name was Wonderful. This is still the name of the parent's God.

* * *

2 Not only does the child in his tenderness and lovingness
call forth the love of your heart; his waywardness and
wilfulness call for it still more, as they put it to the test, and
school it in forbearance and gentleness.

Children that are allowed to be unruly and self-willed will
speedily lose their childlike faith. What is said of men, that
having thrust from them a good conscience they have made
shipwreck of the faith, holds good of children too.

* * *

3 Now with the Bible of God's grace, and then with the
books of God's glory in nature, the whole of the day
and the whole of the life is to be an uninterrupted fellowship
with the Holy One. The continued and spontaneous out-
burstings of the heart, in the language of the life, to prove
that God's presence and love are a reality and a delight. This
is the source: "Thou shalt love the Lord with *all thy* heart,
and the words shall be *in thy heart;* and thou shalt teach
them diligently to thy children, and shalt talk of them when
thou sittest in thine house, and when thou walkest by the
way, when thou liest down, and when thou risest up."

* * *

4 Many parents never understand the truth that to train
for God's service secures the fullest salvation. God says
of Abraham, "I have known him, to the end he may command his children, that they may keep the way of the Lord."

Remember Pharaoh's words, "Go ye, serve the Lord; let your little ones also go with you."

* * *

5 The secret of home rule is self rule, first being ourselves what we want our children to be. A calm stillness of soul that seeks to be guided by God's Spirit is one of the first conditions of success in our own spiritual life, and so in the sacred influence we wish to exert on our children.

* * *

6 Of old, God sought above everything to train His saints to be men of faith. Faith is the soul's surrender to God. It begins with faith in His Word. In an age of doubt and questioning, teach your child to accept what it cannot understand, even what appears mysterious and contrary to reason, because God, who is wise and great, has said it. The child wants to trust, the Word wants to be trusted; let your unfeigned faith bring them into contact.

* * *

7 Christ's healing work is spoken of as the natural result of His atoning work, of which Isaiah had spoken as a bearing of our sickness (Isa. 53; Matt. 8). He left, among the exceeding great and precious promises which are the riches of His Church, the assurance that the prayer of faith would save the sick. He has a thousand times over by His Spirit led His children — applying the promise of His doing whatsoever we will if we abide in Him — to believe and receive the healing of a sick child.

* * *

8 Mother, God gives you this picture of Elizabeth and her child of promise: "Thou shalt have joy and gladness, and many shall rejoice at his birth, for he shall be great in the sight of the Lord," — three marks of a child born under the covering of the Holy Spirit. Among men he may not make a name, in gifts and talents he may not be great, but

great he will be in the sight of Him who sees not as man sees. He will be a vessel God can use for His work, a true way preparer for the coming of the Lord in His kingdom.

* * *

9 "Weep not, she is not dead, but sleepeth." Jesus draws near the lifeless form of each little one over whom a mother's heart is weeping, to remind her that death has been conquered, and that the loved one is not dead in the terrible meaning which sin gave that word, but truly sleeps in that deep and blessed sense which that word now has in His mouth. There is a better life than the life of this earth — the eternal life in which God dwelleth. He took this little one that He might draw thee heavenward, that He might empty thy heart to make more room for Himself, that thou mightest be drawn to Him in thy need, and be prepared for receiving the new revelation He has to give of His power, His love, Himself, and thy life.

* * *

10 The Syrophenician woman believed and triumphed with one weapon, — more prayer, more trust. Mother, pleading for your prodigal child, you have her example, and a thousand words of promise and a revelation of the Father's will and the Saviour's power and love, such as she never had. In the face of all doubts, claim the promise of an answer to prayer in the name of Jesus. Yield yourself to the Holy Spirit, to have everything brought to the light that you must cast out. Trust not the wrestling urgency of your petition; seek your strength in God's promise and faithfulness, in His power and love.

* * *

11 It is as the parents serve God upon the Sabbath, in the beauty of holiness, and as the spirit of holiness breathes on and from them in the services of the Sabbath, as that day is to them, not a day of strict observance, but of joyful worship, of real loving fellowship with God, as it is a delight, that the first condition will be fulfilled for teaching their children to love it.

* * *

12 God's highest gift to creation was His will, that man might choose the will of His God. Obedience is the path to liberty. Parents often say that to develop the will of the child the will must be left free. The will of the child is not free, — passion and prejudice, selfishness and ignorance, seek to influence the child in the wrong direction. Your highest work is to be God's minister in leading your child's will back to His service. To know to refuse the evil and choose the good, will be to choose Christ, and holiness, and eternal life.

* * *

13 It is because the Christian parent too little realises that ruling his house well is a simple matter of duty, a command that must be obeyed, that so many children are ruined by parental weakness. Not to restrain the child is to dishonour God, by honouring the child more than God, because the duty God has imposed is made to give way to the child's will.

* * *

14 "Only believe." Living faith will teach us to see new beauty and preciousness in our children, will waken in us new earnestness and desire, in everything to hold and to train them for God alone. The name of "Faith Home" has been appropriated to certain special institutions; we shall boldly claim it as the name of our own dear home, because everything is done in the faith of Jesus.

* * *

15 God asks and expects us, in doing our work as parents, in every way to copy Him. God's fatherhood is our model and study. In the tenderness, and patience, and self-sacrifice of Divine Love, in the firmness and righteousness of Divine rule, the parent will find the secret of successful training. In a Christian father a child ought to have a better exposition than the best of sermons can give of the love and care of the Heavenly Father, and all the blessing and joy He wants to bestow.

* * *

16 The branch is a perfect likeness of the vine; the only difference is, the one is great and strong, and the source of strength; the other little and feeble, ever needing and receiving strength. Even so the believer is the perfect likeness of Christ *(The True Vine)*.

* * *

17 How can we glorify God? Not by adding to His glory or bringing Him any new glory. In a vine bearing much fruit, the owner is glorified, as it tells of his skill and care. In the disciple who bears much fruit, the Father is glorified. Before men and angels proof is given of the glory of God's grace and power; God's glory shines out through him *(The True Vine)*.

MONEY

18 We ask how much a man *gives;* Christ asks how much he *keeps.* We ask *what* does a man own, *Christ,* how does he use it. The world thinks more about the money getting; Christ about the money giving. The world looks at the money and its amount; Christ at the man and his motive. We look at the gift; Christ asks, was the gift a sacrifice.

* * *

19 If our Lord wanted us to give Him all, like the poor widow who cast her farthing into the treasury, why did He not leave a clear command? That would be the spirit of the world in the Church, looking at *what* we give, at our giving all. We must put all at His feet, as the spontaneous expression of a love, that cannot help giving, just because it loves.

115

20 If we did but see the Lord Jesus in charge of the Heavenly Mint, stamping every true gift and then using it for the kingdom, surely our money would begin to shine with a new lustre. We should begin to say, "The less I can spend on myself, and the more on my Lord, the richer I am." Day by day give, as God blesses and as He asks; it will help to bring heaven nearer to you, and *you* nearer to heaven.

* * *

21 One of the ways of manifesting and maintaining the crucifixion of the flesh, is never to use money to gratify it. The way to conquer every temptation to do so, is to have the heart filled with large thoughts of the spiritual power of money.

How many count themselves really liberal because of what they *will,* while what they *do,* even up to their present means, is not what God would love to see.

* * *

22 When you lie down at night weary, the bed holds you up, and allows you to stretch out your whole body and to rest there. God, the Everlasting One, stretches out His arms and says: "Now, soul, come and rest." He will take you up individually. The Father is very near, not a general Father and God of the Universe, but a special Father for every child of His *(Miscellaneous).*

* * *

23 Do you believe that if God had sent an angel to whisper every moment in your ear, "the Everlasting God is keeping you," you would then have understood how you were to be kept? You have something better than an angel. God has actually given His Holy Spirit into your hearts to keep you always in remembrance of the presence of Jesus, so that you can every minute be kept trusting Him *(Miscellaneous).*

116

24 The experience of the love and the saving power of our incarnate, crucified, glorified Lord, depends entirely upon His indwelling in us to reveal His presence and to do His work. The Lord Jesus brings the heart which accepts and trusts Him to dwell within, into sympathy and harmony with Himself. He becomes your life. He will live in you, and all your thoughts, and tempers, and dispositions, and actions will have His Life and Spirit breathing in them.

* * *

25 Jesus was born twice. The birth at Bethlehem was a birth into a life of weakness. The second time He was born from the grave — "the first born from the dead." Because He gave up His first life that He had by His first birth, God gave Him the life of the second birth in the glory of heaven and the throne of God.

Jesus' heart toward us is all love. His work was, and is, nothing but the revelation of infinite love and tenderness, and nothing but love on our part can be the proof that we have really accepted and known His love.

* * *

26 To do God's will Christ came from heaven; to do God's will in you He has entered your heart. God gave us a will that with it we might intelligently will what He wills.

When Christ comes in to take possession, He will, by His Spirit within, make you what God would have you be — conformable to the image of His Son. Christ's life is altogether too high and too Divine for us to reproduce. It is His own life, and only His, but He will live it out in us.

HAVE MERCY UPON ME

27 Not what a man does or brings, although it is apparently the performance of the law, but the childlike disposition of loving subjection, is the true fulfilling of the law. The worth of our religion depends wholly upon our relation to God.

117

In the midst of all its working and praying, the little child has always the hidden sense of the mother's nearness. The Christian can attain to being so closely knit to his God that in the midst of the severe activities of earth there may always remain the blessed feeling, "My God sees me, and I can look up unto Him."

* * *

28 The joy of forgiveness will not always remain unless it be confirmed as the joy of sanctification. When the first joy began to yield, many a Christian has ascribed the loss to God as a trial which He has sent him. Had he but asked for grace, not only to be washed from guilt, but also to be liberated from the dominion of sin, he would have found that, with the progressive work of grace in the soul, a progressive joy would have been ministered unto him by God.

* * *

29 The more that you cleave to God, and commit yourself to His Word and counsel, the more steadfast shall you stand. Let the Word be your food. Strive by it to think what God thinks, to will what He wills. If the Word of God is thus the rock of your confidence, you will be just as little moved as there is variableness or shadow of turning with God.

* * *

30 The law of God guards the entrance to the gate of heaven. It will let no one within who is not whiter than the snow. "Wash me and I shall be whiter than snow." Nothing less than this God has offered us, nothing less than this can bring us full peace. Alas! how many are seeking peace in their own activity, endeavours, experiences, but they cannot find the stable, full peace which Jesus gives, and which passeth all understanding.

* * *

31 The book of Psalms God offers us as a prayer book, adapted to our need, because the prayers come from

His Spirit, and are therefore Divine; and yet just as genuinely human, because they come from those who are our flesh and blood, and are in everything like ourselves. With the infant class learning the "ABC," the teacher puts the sounds into their mouth. In the Psalms, the Lord God puts into our mouths the very words with which we may come to Him.